TRAINS, JESUS, AND MURDER

THE GOSPEL ACCORDING TO JOHNNY CASH

RICHARD BECK

Fortress Press

Minneapolis

TRAINS, JESUS, AND MURDER
The Gospel according to Johnny Cash

All biblical citations from NIV.

Cover image: Silver Screen Collection/Johnny Cash/Getty Images
Cover design: Lindsey Owens

Print ISBN: 978-1-5064-3376-9
eBook ISBN: 978-1-5064-5559-4

For Jana, Brenden, and Aidan.
You give me cause for love that I cannot hide.

For the men of the Monday-night Bible study
at the French Robertson Unit.
I wish the world could hear us sing.

I love songs about
horses,
railroads,
land,
Judgment Day,
family,
hard times,
whiskey,
courtship,
marriage,
adultery,
separation,
murder,
war,
prison,
rambling,
damnation,
home,
salvation,
death,
pride,
humor,
piety,

rebellion,
patriotism,
larceny,
determination,
tragedy,
rowdiness,
heartbreak
and love.

And Mother.

And God.

—Johnny Cash, liner notes *Unchained*

CONTENTS

CONTENTS

INTRODUCTION

TRAINS, JESUS, AND MURDER

Hello, I'm Johnny Cash."

The brief introduction came through my car speakers, followed by a thunderous eruption so loud that I turned the volume down a bit—hundreds of men cheering, screaming, and stomping their feet. The guitar came in with that signature *boom-chicka-boom* rhythm. And then I heard the iconic, unforgettable voice.

Johnny Cash, live at Folsom Prison.

I was driving to a prison as the Man in Black sang about shooting a man in Reno just to watch him die. Driving past barbed-wire fences, mesquite trees, and cacti, I was heading north out of Abilene, Texas, on Farm Road 1082 to a Texas Department of Criminal Justice facility, the maximum-security French Robertson Unit—home to over two thousand incarcerated souls.

The State of Texas dresses its prisoners in all white. We call the inmates the Men in White. Later I was to discover that Johnny Cash once wrote a book entitled *Man in White*, a novel about the apostle Paul.

1

The music played on: songs of a criminal being hanged ("25 Minutes to Go"), of a man captured and executed for shooting his cheating wife ("Cocaine Blues"), of a prisoner committing suicide ("The Wall"), and of a man released from jail who dies beside the railroad tracks ("Give My Love to Rose"). I'd never heard anything like this concert, and neither had the world when *At Folsom Prison* was released in 1968. Cash sang of murder, suicide, executions, and despair to a raucous audience of inmates behind bars at the infamous Folsom Prison.

At Folsom Prison isn't all dark. The concert is punctuated with fun and lighthearted moments ("Dirty Old Egg-Suckin' Dog," "Flushed from the Bathroom of My Heart"), reflective of Cash's love of joke songs and his desire to bring laughter into the darkness of Folsom. The energy peaks when Cash's wife June comes out to sing "Jackson," a hilarious duet about a couple who got married a bit too impulsively.*

The album ends with the song "Greystone Chapel," written by Glen Sherley, an inmate at Folsom prison. A song about the faith of the incarcerated, "Greystone Chapel" speaks for Folsom inmates searching for the light in their very dark world.

I was driving toward my own Greystone Chapel. On Monday nights, I lead a Bible study for fifty inmates at the French Robertson Unit. Every Monday, I park my car and make my way through security—my person patted down to check for contraband, my Bible scanned in the X-ray machine. I walk past the tall fences topped with razor wire, glancing up at the watchtowers, through the gate and

---

*When I do karaoke with my wife, Jana, "Jackson" is our go-to song. It's a big crowd pleaser.

under the ominous sign that reads, "No Hostages Shall Pass Through This Gate." I move through multiple checkpoints where my ID is verified. Heavy, sliding metal doors lock and unlock, granting me passage and locking me in.

Eventually, I get to the chapel. The correctional officer working the desk calls out my buildings, releasing the men housed in different parts of the facility to come to the study. The Men in White begin to arrive. Officers line them up to be patted down, searching for contraband. Once, an inmate nicknamed "the Philosopher" caused alarm as an officer felt something in his sock. It was a small Bible, one of those pocket New Testaments. The officers put the Philosopher against the wall, patting him down, eventually discovering eight small Bibles hidden all over his person. Some people carry concealed weapons. The guys who come to my Bible study carry concealed Bibles.

Released into the chapel, the men form a reception line. Herb, my coteacher, and I stand and greet each man individually with a warm embrace and a check in. *¿Cómo estás?* How are you? How is your grandmother doing? Did your daughter write you back? How is your health? Was a date for the parole hearing set?

For many of the Men in White, this greeting time is the highlight of their week. Many of the inmates don't get visitors, having no family to speak of. For these men, we are the only people from "the free world" who come to see them. For their entire week, our embrace and conversation are the only experience they will have during which they can forget they are a prisoner.

I bought Johnny Cash's *At Folsom Prison* because of these men. I had been leading the study for a few years when I came across the album at a music store. I knew it was a live concert Cash had recorded inside Folsom. My experiences at French Robertson drew me to the album. I bought it, figuring it would be a great thing to listen to as I drove out of town on country roads toward the prison each week.

I didn't know much about Johnny Cash at the time, but I knew a bit. Even if you're not a fan, it's hard not to know a few things about Johnny Cash, sort of like how everyone knows something about Elvis—that he was "the King of Rock and Roll"—and can probably sing along to "You Ain't Nothing but a Hound Dog." In a similar way, most people have heard Johnny Cash referred to as "the Man in Black" and have heard the songs "I Walk the Line" and "Ring of Fire." Maybe you saw the movie *I Walk the Line,* starring Joaquin Phoenix and Reese Witherspoon as Johnny Cash and June Carter. That's about as much as I knew of Johnny Cash when I popped in *At Folsom Prison* for the first time during my drive out to the prison.

The second I heard the Folsom inmates scream after Cash's standard concert opening ("Hello, I'm Johnny Cash"), I was hooked. What captivated me about the album wasn't just Cash's grim song selection, the cussing, the complaints about the prison water, or the banter with the guards and prisoners. It was the sound of the room—the inmates cheering, hollering out, and laughing. I listened to the officers breaking in between songs: "I have an announcement here: 88419 is wanted in reception." The voices of inmates, the prisoner ID numbers being called out, guards interrupting, the just-under-the-surface tension between the officers and the inmates, booing the warden—I know that world. I step into it every Monday night.

Beyond that flash of recognition, I was also transfixed by the contrasts of the concert. Murder ballads were juxtaposed with hymns of faith. That clash between the darkness and the light drew me deeper into the music of Johnny Cash. In 2000, Cash released a compilation set titled *Love, God, Murder*. Disc 1 is filled with love songs from "I Walk the Line" to "I Still Miss Someone." Disc 2 is bursting with gospel songs—some old standards like "Were You There (When They Crucified My Lord)?" and "Swing Low, Sweet Chariot," but also many, including "Redemption," written by Cash. Finally, Disc 3, *Murder*, is dripping with blood and stuffed with murder ballads, from the chilling "Delia's Gone" to the dark romp "Cocaine Blues." The liner notes to *Murder* perfectly capture the darkness that threads its way through Cash's music: "With their brutal sheriffs, pitiless judges, cheatin' tramps, escaped fugitives, condemned men, chain gang prisoners, unjustly accused innocents, and first-person protagonist who'd shoot a man just to watch him die, Cash songs . . . are poems to the criminal mentality."[1]

My son Aidan, who has listened to a lot of Johnny Cash music because of me, once quipped, "Johnny Cash sings about three things: trains, Jesus, and murder."

Trains, Jesus, and murder. That's not a bad summary of the music of Johnny Cash.

That contrast between Jesus and murder, between gospel hymns and odes to a criminal mentality—and there is nothing like this contrast in the whole of the music industry—is what fascinated me about the music of Johnny Cash. As John Carter Cash observed about his father's music, Johnny Cash "got people's attention with songs like 'Cocaine Blues' or 'Folsom Prison Blues,' his demeanor cool and dark. Then he professed his faith and sang of God and salvation."[2] Sure, there are artists out there, from rappers to metal bands, who sing about thugs and killing. And plenty of Jesus music is being pumped out by the Christian music industry. But no one sings about Jesus and murder on the very same album. No one, that is, except Johnny Cash.

Pick up any Johnny Cash album, and you'll likely find a hymn of praise next to a murder ballad. Saints and sinners are all jumbled up together. This is the mixture I discovered out at the prison: "Cocaine Blues" and "Greystone Chapel" are found in the very same place or person. Seams of gold run through the blackest of hearts. Faith shines brightest in the darkest of places. And I feel closest to God worshipping with the damned.

These are contrasts that transfix us about the music and life of Johnny Cash. Rosanne Cash aptly captures the startling juxtapositions, contrasts, and paradoxes of her father and his art: "His heart was so expansive and his mind so finely tuned that he could contain both darkness and light, love and trouble, fear and faith, wholeness and shatteredness, old-school and postmodern, the sacred and the silly, God and the Void. He was a Baptist with the soul of a mystic. He was a poet who worked in the dirt. He was an enlightened being who was wracked with the suffering of addiction and grief."[3]

The author Flannery O'Connor once said her literary project was describing the action of grace in territory controlled by the devil. The same can be said about the music of Johnny Cash. It's what I've experienced with the Men in White on Monday evenings: the action of grace in territory controlled by the devil, Jesus among the murderers, the saint within the sinner, God in the depths of hell.

Trains, Jesus, and murder—somewhere in there is the gospel according to Johnny Cash.

PART 1

FAMILY AND FAITH

CHAPTER 1

"I AM BOUND FOR THE PROMISED LAND"

As J.R.'s brother Jack lay delirious and dying, he saw himself standing by a river, gazing into the heavenly city, where the streets were paved with gold. "Can you hear the angels singing?" Jack asked as he clutched his mother's hand. "What a beautiful city. And the angels singing. Oh mama, I wish you could hear the angels singing."[1] And with those words, Jack died.

———

Johnny Cash's love of gospel music was rooted in the Arkansas dirt, but his evangelistic passion for singing gospel music was born out of family tragedy. Jack's death made Johnny Cash a preacher.

J. R. Cash was born on February 26, 1932, in Kingsland, Arkansas, to Ray and Carrie Cash. (In the Air Force, J.R. started going by "John," and it was Sun Records that started calling their rockabilly star "Johnny" to appeal to the teenagers who were swooning over that other Sun star, Elvis Presley.) The fourth of seven children, J.R. had two older brothers, Roy and Jack, each of whom would play pivotal roles in his life. Roy was the eldest Cash child and would eventually introduce J.R. to Luther Perkins and Marshall Grant. And Jack was J.R.'s best friend.

In 1935, when little J.R. was three, Ray Cash moved the family to Dyess, Arkansas, a New Deal government-assisted colony where struggling farmers were given a house, a stipend, and twenty acres of land to clear and cultivate. The Cash family moved into house number 226 on Road 3. Ray quickly began to clear the land for cotton planting. In the years to come, J.R. joined in the family work of picking cotton. The scars he carried on his fingers from the sharp cotton burrs—the stigmata of cotton farming—would always remind him of his humble roots. In addition to pricked and bleeding fingers, life in Dyess was punctuated by poverty and pain. The family struggled through the Great Depression. And twice the Mississippi River flooded the farm, an experience captured by Cash in his song "Five Feet High and Rising," in which a child keeps track of the floodwaters by repeatedly asking his mother how high the water has risen.

Cash sang about life in Dyess throughout his career. His song "Country Boy" expresses the joy of a boy fishing and hunting after he's been set free from hoeing the fields. The song appears on Cash's very first album with Sun Records, *Johnny Cash and His Hot and Blue Guitar*, and again on one of his last, *Unchained*, recorded with the famous producer Rick Rubin. Those bookends serve as a fitting tribute to a childhood lived in the cotton fields of Arkansas. From start to finish, J.R. was a country boy.

Music eased the pain of those hard Depression years, and gospel music was a passion J.R. shared with his mother, Carrie. Cash's first memories of music were of singing gospel hymns with his family while they picked cotton in their fields and sitting at the feet of his mother as she sang out of a Baptist hymnal. The first song Cash could remember was the hymn "I Am Bound for the Promised Land":

On Jordan's stormy banks I stand,
And cast a wishful eye
To Canaan's fair and happy land,
Where my possessions lie.

I am bound for the promised land,
I am bound for the promised land;
Oh, who will come and go with me?
I am bound for the promised land.

Cash sang songs like "I'll Fly Away" and "Softly and Tenderly" to himself almost every day of his life, and they endured as his favorite form of prayer. The last gospel album released by Cash, a year after his death, was fittingly titled *My Mother's Hymnbook*, a nostalgic collection of all the songs Cash had learned from his mother, including "I'm Bound for the Promised Land." The sound of the album is simple and spare, just Cash accompanying himself on acoustic guitar, the way the hymns would have sounded during his Dyess childhood. In the liner notes, he declared that, of all his many albums, *My Mother's Hymnbook* was his favorite. As John Carter Cash observed about his father, "Gospel music fed his spirit and was essential to the formation of my father's Christian faith."[2]

—

I grew up singing these same songs in the Churches of Christ, a faith tradition that worships by singing unaccompanied four-part harmony out of hymnals. Some of my earliest and fondest memories are sultry summer evenings, sitting in the pews with about thirty other members of the congregation. Once a month, we'd devote the evening exclusively to singing. From the pews, we'd call out numbers in the hymnal to the song leader. I preferred weepers in minor keys like "O Sacred Head" over up-tempo numbers like "Sing and Be Happy." Calling out the numbers of favorite hymns is the first memory I have of speaking and participating in Christian community.

Many Churches of Christ have moved on from our a cappella, four-part harmony and hymnal-based tradition, opting for praise bands and songs published by the Christian worship industry. Much of this new music moves me, but it doesn't penetrate to the deepest levels of my soul, as "Amazing Grace" and "To Canaan's Land I'm On My Way" do. Like Johnny Cash, I find that my love language with God is an old gospel hymn.

I've reconnected with these hymns on Monday nights at the prison. In the early months of leading the Bible study, I'd noticed hymnals filling a couple of shelves in the prison chapel. "Do you ever use these?" I asked the Men in White.

"No," they replied, "No one knows any of the songs."

"Well, I do," I said. "Let's pass those hymnals out."

That started our Monday-night tradition of passing out the hymnals midway through the study to have a good old-fashioned hymn sing, with the Men in White calling out numbers and us launching into a hymn. And over the years, I'm happy to report, our harmonies have gotten pretty good. Some nights, we keep singing and singing, not stopping until the guards interrupt to tell us our time is up.

When Cash started his music career, he thought he'd become a gospel singer. Cash wanted to sing gospel music because he had made a promise to his brother Jack. In 1944, when J.R. was twelve, tragedy struck the Cash family when Jack was killed in a horrific accident with an electric saw; he was pulled into the saw and almost cut in half. Jack lingered painfully for a week before he died. He was fifteen.

The morning of the accident, J.R. had tried to get Jack to go fishing with him. Jack declined, choosing instead to earn a little money for the family by making fence posts at the high school. J.R. pleaded with Jack to come fishing, and years later Cash shared that he'd had an ominous feeling that day, dreading that something bad was going to happen to Jack. But Jack felt he had an obligation to earn some money to help the family.

After fishing for a few hours, J.R. began walking home. He saw the preacher's car approaching with his father inside. That was strange; something was wrong. When they pulled up, Ray Cash said to J.R, "Throw away your fishin' pole and get in." As they drove, Ray finally shared what had happened, "Jack's been hurt awfully bad."[3]

When they got to the house, Ray Cash grabbed a blood-soaked paper bag that contained Jack's torn and bloody clothes. "Come out to the smokehouse, J.R. I want to show you," said Ray. Once in the smokehouse, Ray laid out Jack's khaki pants, belt, shirt, and shoes. The pants had been cut from the rib cage down to the pelvis, cutting the belt in two. Staring at the torn, bloody clothes and marking the route the saw tore through Jack's abdomen, Ray Cash began to cry. Trembling and traumatized, young J.R. stumbled out of the smokehouse.

The reasons why Ray Cash felt the need to show Jack's torn and bloody clothing to a twelve-year-old are hard to fathom. For some reason, as became clear later on, Ray Cash felt that J.R. was responsible, at least partly, for Jack's death. Cash internalized this blame and was haunted by guilt his entire life, making himself responsible for failing to convince Jack to go fishing with him that day.

Jack had been the pride and joy of the Cash family. He was smart, handsome, friendly, and kind. Deeply religious, Jack had declared that he was going to become a preacher. As John Carter Cash observed, "Jack was Dad's best friend, and Dad looked up to him. Jack was strong and full of the love for God. He aspired at an early age to become a pastor and was on his way, studying the Bible daily."[4]

The day Jack died, J.R. went to the cemetery and helped dig his brother's grave. During the funeral service, the dirt from Jack's grave still covered him. And in many ways, that dirt clung to Johnny Cash for the rest of his life.

Filled with grief and guilt over Jack's death, J.R. withdrew into himself. He started taking long, solitary walks at night, singing to himself. One night, he had an epiphany. He'd been thinking for weeks about how to keep Jack's memory alive. He had even toyed with becoming a minister himself to honor Jack. And then one night, as he sang gospel hymns to himself underneath the stars, a revelation came to him: he would spread Jack's message by singing gospel music.

———

Cash kept his promise to Jack. He became the preacher Jack never would, performing and recording gospel music for his entire career. He even wrote and produced *The Gospel Road*, a 1973 movie accompanied by a double album, about the life of Jesus.

However, the guilt over Jack's death and the blame of his father wounded Cash in deep and lasting ways. The demons of self-destruction that Cash battled throughout his life, most notably a drug addiction, were likely rooted in the traumas of his childhood. Sadness and darkness became permanent features of his personality and found their way into his music. The paradoxes and contradictions that transfix us about Johnny Cash—the jarring mixture of light and dark, saint and sinner—all flow out of the trauma of Jack's death. Gospel music became mixed with shadows. "Amazing Grace" bled into "Folsom Prison Blues." Cash's daughter Rosanne summed it up well: "Dad was wounded so profoundly by Jack's death, and by his father's reaction—the blame and recrimination and bitterness. If someone survives that kind of damage, either great evil or great art can come out of it. And my dad had the seed of great art in him."[5]

For the rest of his life, Jack was never far from Cash's mind. At the end of his 1975 autobiography, *Man in Black*, Cash is on a plane flying to meet his family. As he does so often, he's thinking about Jack. And then, out of nowhere, the plane hits a massive air pocket—a violent bit of turbulence that knocks everyone's coffee off the seat trays. Curious about the source of the turbulence, Cash looks out the window. He recounts:

I looked out the window again, and way off to my right was Memphis, Tennessee, about forty miles away. And then a chill went over me, because I knew *exactly* where we were.

Straight down beneath me from that plane was a little patch of green—the Bassett Cemetery where my brother Jack was buried. Tears came to my eyes. . . .

The instant we hit that bump, we had been directly over Jack's grave at Bassett, Arkansas. . . . The bump was one of those beautiful "my cup runneth over" kind of blessings. It was a spiritual "high" which only comes once in a great while for me.

I looked down at that little cemetery plot fading back into the horizon, and I smiled and whispered, "Hey, Jack! I'm still singing those hymns you and I loved so much. . . .

And by the way—I'll see you later, Jack."[6]

That's the gospel as Johnny Cash learned it singing hymns while picking cotton with his family in Arkansas: we are all bound for the promised land.

Johnny Cash had to trick Sam Phillips into recording his first gospel song. The head of Sun Records in Memphis, Tennessee, knew what the kids wanted to hear from the jukeboxes. Phillips knew this because Sun's biggest star, a kid from Tupelo, Mississippi, named Elvis Aaron Presley, was making his splash with energetic, upbeat songs like "That's Alright" and "Good Rockin' Tonight," songs that got the teenagers dancing at sock hops. This music came to be known as rockabilly—a mixture of rhythm and blues with country ("hillbilly") music—one of the early sounds of what would later be called "rock 'n' roll." So although Johnny Cash came to Sun wanting to be a gospel singer, Sam Phillips had other ideas: he wanted Cash to be his next Elvis.

In 1954, Cash had moved to Memphis with his new wife, Vivian. Now going by John, he had just finished a four-year stint in the Air

Force, working as a radio operator in Europe. John had met Vivian at a roller-skating rink in 1951, right before his deployment. A long-distance relationship ensued, and a month after his discharge, John and Vivian married.

The couple moved to Memphis to be near Roy Cash, and John started a job selling kitchen appliances. Roy worked at a car dealership, where he introduced his younger brother to two of his coworkers, Luther Perkins and Marshall Grant. Along with Cash, Perkins and Grant were into music, and the three started getting together to play in the evenings. John played rhythm guitar, Perkins bought a Fender, and Grant picked up a used stand-up bass. They weren't very talented musicians. Grant, who had no experience with the bass, had to put tape on the neck of the instrument to find the notes. Perkins picked his notes out on the Fender slowly and deliberately, one by one. But during their evenings together, they developed a simple but distinctive sound: a *boom-chicka-boom* rhythm. It was a steady, driving beat that sounded like the clickety-clack of a train, the perfect contrast for John's clear, forceful, bass-baritone voice.

After being hounded by Cash, Sam Phillips eventually allowed the group to audition for him. Phillips was intrigued by their spare, unique sound—the combo of a clickety-clack rhythm with a voice that hit you like a freight train. The trio mainly performed gospel songs for Phillips, but Sam dismissed that material. Phillips did, however, like one of the songs that John had written while in the Air Force. A song about a man coming home after being discharged from the service, "Hey, Porter!" had the fast tempo Phillips was looking for. Phillips sent the group back home to write another rockabilly song for the B side of the record. They returned with "Cry, Cry, Cry!"

They cut a record, and in May 1955, the radio stations of Memphis introduced "Johnny Cash and the Tennessee Two" to the world.

The timing was perfect for Sun Records. Elvis would leave Sun for RCA the following year. Johnny Cash and the Tennessee Two stepped in to fill the gap, becoming a workhorse for Sun, which eventually added other stars, including Jerry Lee Lewis and Roy Orbison, to their lineup. During his years with Sun Records, Cash recorded lots of rockabilly music for Sam Phillips, including "Get Rhythm," "Ballad of a Teenage Queen," and "Luther Played the Boogie."

If you like Cash in upbeat, rockabilly mode—and I do—it doesn't get any better than the Sun years. But much of this teenybopper music feels incongruous coming from the man who would later cuss his way through *At Folsom Prison* in a room full of murderers. Still, the darker side of Cash's music did make an appearance early on in the Sun years. "Folsom Prison Blues," with its chilling reference to killing a man in Reno just to watch him die, was recorded for Sun in 1955, and the tragic ballad of poverty and loss "Give My Love to Rose" was recorded in 1957. These were harbingers of the music to come.

———

During those early years at Sun, Cash never let go of his desire to record gospel music and stay true to his promise to his dead brother. So Cash kept pushing. And Phillips kept resisting. It became a point of tension, and Cash eventually left Sun to sign with Columbia Records in 1958. Given greater creative freedom at Columbia, Cash was finally able to release his first full gospel album, *Hymns by Johnny Cash*.

But Cash did figure out a way to sneak a gospel song past Sam Phillips—and probably past you as well. After Cash debuted with "Hey, Porter!" and "Cry, Cry, Cry!" his career at Sun Records began to take off. The royalty checks started coming in, and the heavy touring began. Cash quit his job selling appliances, which he was never very good at anyway, and moved Vivian to a bigger house. Johnny Cash was becoming a rock star.

But with music success came domestic stress. Vivian wanted a tranquil and conventional domestic life. And while the money was nice, she had no desire to be married to a rock 'n' roller. John, for his part, very much wanted to be a music star. As he grew more successful, their visions of the future diverged. Vivian wanted John at home, and John wanted to be in the studio or on the road, playing to bigger and bigger crowds. Vivian also worried about John's faithfulness to their wedding vows. She'd seen how the young girls were responding to Elvis, so she had reason to be worried. Wanting to reassure Vivian, Cash composed for her an ode to fidelity, "I Walk the Line":

> I keep a close watch on this heart of mine
> I keep my eyes wide open all the time
> I keep the ends out for the tie that binds
> Because you're mine, I walk the line.

I don't know how reassured Vivian was by "I Walk the Line," but Sam Phillips loved the song. However, there was one problem. Wanting "I Walk the Line" to be a romantic love ballad for his worried wife, Cash sang the song slowly, even sadly. Always searching for that rockabilly beat, Phillips kept telling Cash to push the tempo during the recording session. Cash refused. But at very end of the session, on a lark, Phillips got Cash to record one final take of "I Walk the Line" with an up-tempo beat. Cash sang it fast, but he assumed Phillips was going to release the version they had worked on during the entire session—the slower ballad.

So Cash was more than a bit shocked when he heard "I Walk the Line" on the radio for the first time. Phillips had released the up-tempo version. Furious, Cash angrily confronted Sam. But the hard feelings quickly subsided when it became clear that "I Walk the Line" was a hit, a huge hit—the greatest hit, in fact, of Cash's career.

While Sam Phillips might have pulled one over on Cash with "I Walk the Line," Cash also had managed to pull one over on Phillips. Johnny snuck in a gospel tune without Sam knowing it. "I Walk the Line" is really a crypto-gospel song, a song with two meanings. Intended to be, in the words of Robert Hilburn, "an expression of spiritual as well as romantic allegiance,"[1] the song can be understood as a pledge of faithfulness not only to the singer's spouse but also to God. During an interview just months before his death, Cash shared, "Sam never knew it, but 'I Walk the Line' was my first gospel hit."[2]

———

The irony is that Cash didn't keep his promise to Vivian—nor to God, for that matter. And the infidelities were linked. During the sixties, Cash's marriage to Vivian deteriorated, despite their having four daughters during those years—Rosanne, Kathy, Cindy, and Tara. During the same period, Cash grew increasingly addicted to amphetamines. Having promised to "walk the line" for Vivian and God, he drifted away from both. Concerning "I Walk the Line,"

Mikal Gilmore observes that the song "claimed an impossible ideal for Cash. He was not an unswerving man. In fact, he strayed a lot—into rebellion, into abject addictions, into faithlessness of many sorts."[3] Cash's close friend Merle Haggard agrees: "Johnny Cash was out of line all his life. 'I Walk the Line' was kind of ludicrous for him to sing. . . . He never walked any line."[4]

All the broken promises fed into and fueled each other. Cash felt guilty for being an unfaithful husband and for not being a better father to his girls, given how often he was away from home. The pills helped him escape the feelings of guilt, but they also pulled him away from his family, which led to more guilt, which led to more pills. Moral and psychological problems frequently take the form of these negative feedback loops, and Cash was caught in one—a reinforcing, spiraling, and self-destructive cycle that led him deeper and deeper into hell.

———

Hell arrived for Johnny Cash in 1967, the darkest year of his life. Vivian finalized their divorce, and Cash's addiction brought him to the brink of suicide.

But if the gospel according to Johnny Cash is anything, it's really not about our ability to walk the line. The gospel isn't about our faithfulness to God; it's about God's faithfulness to us. Johnny Cash couldn't walk the line. Nor can you or I or anyone else. God walks the line for us.

In the pit of hell, grace found Johnny Cash. Much of that grace came to him in the form of June Carter, the love of his life. From a tomb of darkness, June walked Cash back into the light. By all accounts, June saved Johnny. And although Vivian would always nurse pain, she and Cash eventually reconciled. Late in his life, Vivian wrote a memoir of their romance and marriage, sharing personal details from that painful season of their lives. Although widely respected as a Christian role model and family man, Cash knew it was time to share some of the darker aspects of his life. And Vivian needed to share her side of the story. He blessed her memoir, and it was published. Cash also went on to reconcile with his daughters, who for years, like so many children of divorce, felt torn between their two parents.

The word that describes the faithfulness of God in the Hebrew Scriptures is *hesed*, referring to God's covenantal loyalty, kindness, and fidelity to God's people. *Hesed* is God singing "I Walk the Line" to us.

We find two covenants in the Hebrew Bible. One of them is the covenant God makes with Israel on Mount Sinai, giving the law that contains the Ten Commandments. It is a covenant of rewards and punishments. At the end of his life, Moses famously describes the choice facing God's people: "Today I set before you life and death" (Deuteronomy 30:19, paraphrase). If we're faithful to God, if we walk the line, blessings will abound to us. But if we fail to walk the line, there will be hell to pay.

Like Johnny Cash, Israel failed to walk the line, so they faced consequences. And as specified in the Sinai covenant, the consequence was exile. The story, at this point, seems to come to its sad, predictable conclusion. We made a promise. We broke our promise. We get what we deserve. The end. In 1967, Johnny Cash found himself at this dead end. And today, during our Monday nights at the prison, that's the story of the Men in White. They've made their mistakes, and now they are paying for them. As it was for Israel, sitting in exile, their story seems to be over.

And then, out of nowhere, grace surprises us.

Remember, there were *two* covenants in the life of Israel. Before Mount Sinai, there was an earlier covenant—the deeper, primordial covenant that God had made with Abraham. And in contrast with Mount Sinai, this primordial covenant was a covenant that God—and God alone—initiated, created, and assumed the burden of.

A famous scene in Genesis 15 describes God establishing the covenant with Abraham. God makes a promise to Abraham, to bless him and to make him a great nation. To make this a binding promise and agreement, the custom of that time was to cut animals in half and then have the two parties walk the path between them, literally "walking the line" between the animals. The idea is roughly to say, "Let this happen to me—let me be cut in two, if I break my promise to you."

So God asks Abraham to get a heifer, a goat, a ram, a dove, and a pigeon and then prepare them for the covenantal ceremony. Abraham divides the animals and then lays them out, preparing the path. Abraham waits and then falls into a deep sleep. The sun sets, and darkness falls. God then appears in the form of a light—a flaming torch. The light proceeds to move down the path, walking the binding, covenantal line between the animals.

What's strange and shocking about this story in Genesis 15 is that only God walks the line. Normally, both parties of a covenantal agreement were obligated to walk the path between the animals. But in Genesis 15, only God walks the path; Abraham never does. Unlike the covenant on Mount Sinai, where Israel had to make promises and keep up its side of the deal, the primordial covenant God makes with Abraham and Israel is wholly one-sided. Abraham and Israel have neither the ability nor responsibility to maintain this covenant. This deeper covenant is solely and purely the product of God's *hesed*, God walking the line for us. In the words of the old hymn, this is a love that will not let you go, no matter how badly you screw it up.

And this is the covenant that surprises Israel in the midst of being in exile. You might get what you deserve, but that's never the end of your story—not with God. When all hope is lost and when it has finally hit the fan, a song of grace comes to us. We may have broken faith with God, but God will never, ever break faith with us. And so, in the midst of exile, Israel hears this song:

How can I give you up, Ephraim?
How can I hand you over, Israel?
(Hosea 11:8)

That is the gospel of God's *hesed*—God never giving up on us, God's fidelity and faithfulness to the deeper covenant, even when we screw it all up (and especially when we screw it all up).

This is the song the Men in White and I keep singing during our hymn sings out at the prison on Monday nights, and most nights we can't stop singing. Your story, sings grace to the Men in White, is not over. Almost every week, we sing "Amazing Grace":

Through many dangers, toils, and snares
I have already come;
'Tis grace that brought me safe thus far
And grace will lead me home.

As Johnny Cash once shared about those years of addiction and spiritual rebellion, "The times when I was so down and out of it were also the times when I felt the presence of God. . . . I felt that presence, that positive power saying to me, 'I'm still here.'"[5]

I am still here. *Hesed.* That is the gospel according to Johnny Cash: God walking the line for us.

PART 2

SINNERS AND SOLIDARITY

CHAPTER 3

"THE MAN IN BLACK"

The first place to look for Christ is in Hell."[1] That's William Stringfellow's suggestion about where to start looking for God in the world, and it's a perfect description of the gospel according to the Man in Black.

Cash's choice of black attire started early in his career, at his very first public performance. The first time Johnny Cash, Luther Perkins, and Marshall Grant performed for an audience was at a church in North Memphis. One of their neighbors had asked if the trio would like to do a few gospel songs for their Sunday-evening service. The group agreed but got stuck on what to wear. No one owned a suit, and the only colored shirts they had in common were black, so that's what they wore. Black became Cash's sartorial preference for the rest of his career, becoming an iconic part of his image.

For that first gig, Cash quipped, "Black is better for church." He repeated that joke over the years, but fans haven't associated Cash's black dress with church. The Man in Black is, instead, an outlaw image, a part of the outlaw movement Cash pioneered in country music, along with artists like Willie Nelson and Waylon Jennings. So which is it? Is the Man in Black a man of God or an outlaw? The answer is both—the classic Johnny Cash paradox. As Bono, the lead singer of U2, said about Cash, "Johnny Cash doesn't sing to the damned, he sings with the damned, and sometimes you feel he might prefer their company."[2]

———

If the gospel according to Johnny Cash is anything, it's standing with the outcasts and outlaws of the world. Johnny Cash spoke for the underdog, the forgotten, and the ignored. Jesus was notorious for hanging out with sinners and prostitutes. Cash's music followed suit. As James Hetfield, from the heavy-metal band Metallica, said about Cash: "He's speaking for the broken people—people who can't speak up or no one wants to hear."[3] It was not unlike Jesus touching the lepers.

Cash formalized the association between the Man in Black and the outcasts of the world in his signature song. First performed publicly in 1970 before a college audience at Vanderbilt University, "The Man in Black" describes how Cash dons black clothing as a symbol of grief and protest for the oppressed and victimized:

I wear the black for the poor and the beaten down
Livin' in the hopeless, hungry side of town.

The song is both protest and lament as Cash goes through a litany of suffering. In the lyrics, Cash stands in solidarity with the poor, the hungry, the hopeless, the addicts, the elderly, the incarcerated, the abandoned, the beaten down, and the forgotten soldier killed in war (Vietnam was raging at the time).

Beyond radio airplay, the biggest impact of "The Man in Black" was upon the musical variety show Cash was hosting at the time. Living into the ideals he expressed in the song, Cash used *The Johnny Cash Show* to speak directly into many of the divisions ripping the country apart, then as now. For example, he used the show to challenge the racial prejudices within the country music industry and his southern fan base by inviting black artists, among them Stevie Wonder and Louis Armstrong, to the hallowed and historic Ryman Auditorium stage.

The gospel according to the Man in Black is a gospel rooted in *solidarity*. The cross of Christ, in this view, is an act of divine identification with the oppressed. On the cross, God is found with and among the victims of the world. More, given that crucified persons were considered to be cursed by God—"Cursed is anyone who is hung upon a tree" (Deuteronomy 21:23)—God is found in Jesus among the cursed and godforsaken. Again, the first place to look for Jesus is in hell.

By standing with the poor and beaten down, the music of Johnny Cash shows us how a gospel of solidarity begins as an interpretative activity: the cross is a way of seeing and reading the world. Specifically, the cross helps us answer this most important question: Where is God? Here's how Dietrich Bonhoeffer described the way divine solidarity helps us locate God in the world:

> God is not ashamed of human lowliness but goes right into
> the middle of it. . . . God draws near to the lowly, loving

the lost, the unnoticed, the unremarkable, the excluded, the powerless, and the broken. What people say is lost, God says is found; what people say is "condemned," God says is "saved." Where people say No! God says Yes! Where people turn their eyes away in indifference or arrogance, God gazes with a love that grows warmer there than anywhere else. Where people say something is despicable, God calls it blessed.[4]

That is the gospel according to the Man in Black: drawing near to and loving the lost, unnoticed, unremarkable, excluded, powerless, broken, condemned, and despicable. Solidarity is a love that grows warmest in the coldest places.

That vision prompts us to take the second step in the dance of divine solidarity. After we read the world to locate God among the victims and the oppressed, we are called to action, to move ourselves to stand with those who are suffering. As Bonheoffer said, God "goes right into the middle of it." God draws near.

Love moves. Love doesn't stand in place. Solidarity implies involvement. Often, this involvement means physically relocating yourself in the world, to move and stand in a different spot, to find yourself among a different group of people. Solidarity is more than a hashtag or a Facebook post. This is why Cash started performing concerts in prisons, and it's the reason I spend Monday nights with the Men in White. To express solidarity, I needed to put myself in a different physical location.

Try this simple test of solidarity: Look to your left and your right and ask, "Are these people different from me?" If not, think about moving. I like how Ched Myers puts it: "After all the heavy breathing we do about God, it's quite simply where one places one's body that really counts. In other words, what part of town you live in, who you hang out with, who you work alongside. And above all how many social boundaries you cross in order to be with Jesus."[5] Or, more simply, Myers goes on to say, "Hope is where your ass is."

CHAPTER 4

"FOLSOM PRISON BLUES"

I just want to tell you that this show is being recorded for an album release with Columbia Records, and you can't say hell or shit or anything like that.

—Johnny Cash, *At Folsom Prison*[1]

Cash had started playing prison concerts about ten years before recording *At Folsom Prison*. His first prison show, in 1959, was in Huntsville, Texas. A thunderstorm hit during the outdoor show, soaking the performers and causing a power outage. Without amplification, the inmates couldn't hear Cash play, so they disobeyed the orders to stay in their seats and moved to the foot of the stage. What should have been a disaster proved to be a revelation. The enthusiasm and the gratitude from the inmates overwhelmed Cash. The connection he felt with the audience was electric. He'd never experienced anything like it.

Moved by the reception he had received at Huntsville, Cash quickly scheduled another concert at the notorious San Quentin

State Prison. Over the next decade, Cash played more than thirty prison shows, each without compensation. And what he observed during those shows pricked his heart and fueled his activism in the seventies when he called for prison reform. When pushed about why his attention focused on the men in prison rather than upon the victims, Cash once said, "People say, 'well what about the victims, the people that suffer—you're always talking about the prisoners: what about the victims?' Well, the point I want to make is that's what I've always been concerned about—the victims. If we make better men out of the men in prison, then we've got less crime on the streets, and my family and yours is safer when they come out."[2]

The origin of the song "Folsom Prison Blues," which had such huge appeal to his prison audiences (at that first concert in Huntsville, the inmates demanded that he sing it twice), dated back to Cash's years in the Air Force. During his first month stationed in Germany, he saw the film *Inside the Walls of Folsom Prison* at the base movie theater. The film made such an impression that he started toying with a song about life in prison. Soon after, he heard "Crescent City Blues," a haunting song that captured Cash's imagination. Giving voice to the loneliness Cash was experiencing at the time, "Crescent City Blues" reminded him of the alienation of the prisoners in *Inside the Walls of Folsom Prison*. Leaning heavily on the lyrics of "Crescent City Blues," Cash worked to bring the film and song together. The result was "Folsom Prison Blues":

I hear the train a comin'
It's rollin' 'round the bend,
And I ain't seen the sunshine
Since, I don't know when
I'm stuck in Folsom Prison
And time keeps draggin' on
But that train keeps a-rollin'
On down to San Antone.

Although it wasn't the first recorded or released, "Folsom Prison Blues" was one of the first songs Cash played for Sam Phillips. The song marked Cash, right from the start of his career, as a different sort of artist. He had approached Phillips wanting to record gospel music; yet here was this dark, sad song with an offhand reference to a cold-blooded murder:

But I shot a man in Reno
Just to watch him die.

There was something dark and dangerous about Johnny Cash. Which is, let's admit, a strange vibe for an aspiring gospel singer.

It's that juxtaposition—Jesus and murder—that makes Johnny Cash so compelling. Marshall Grant noted the contrast between "Folsom Prison Blues" and the teenybopper music dominating the airwaves at the time: "Everyone sang about love; not everyone sang about shooting a man 'just to watch him die.' I didn't know if you could even put that in a song. As soon as I heard it, I remember asking, 'John, are you sure they'll play something like that on the radio?'"[3] There's a sociopathic edge to that line, even by modern standards. But what really appealed to Cash's prison audiences about the song was the way it spoke to their loneliness and alienation. The imagery of the song centers on an inmate listening to the sound of a passing train, which represents a lost freedom: the sound of the whistle, signaling happy people off to happy places, highlights the plight of the incarcerated singer. Alone and stuck in a prison cell, the prisoner listens to the train rumbling past, carrying people away to joy-filled destinations. That contrast between singer and train, between incarceration and freedom, is the ache of the song, evoking loss, alienation, guilt, and longing.

Despite the cold-blooded reference to murder, at its heart "Folsom Prison Blues" sings of sorrow and regret, the very element that sets Cash's murder ballads apart from the violence found in much of contemporary music. As Quentin Tarantino observes about Cash's murder ballads:

Cash sings tales of men trying to escape. Escape from the law, escape from the poverty they were born into, escape prison, escape madness, escape the people who torture them. But one thing Cash never lets them escape is regret. Unlike most gangsta rap, Cash's criminal life songs rarely take place during the high times. In fact, most songs take place after the cell door has slammed shut or a judge's gavel has condemned a man to death.

When a man faces a rope or 99 years in a cage for the choices he made, when he tells the story of those choices, he tells it not with bravado, but an overwhelming sense of regret.

Sun released "Folsom Prison Blues" in 1957, and it became one of Cash's most iconic songs, along with "I Walk the Line." And those two songs varied in their popularity depending upon Cash's audience. As Michael Streissguth comments, "On the outside [of prison], at the country fairs and nightclubs, they cried for 'I Walk the Line.' Inside, the anthem was 'Folsom Prison Blues.'"[4] As Cash himself observed, "'After 'Folsom Prison Blues,' the prisoners felt kinda like I was one of them. I'd get letters from them, some asking for me to come and play."[5]

Yet, despite the song's focus on a prisoner, the guilt and regret expressed in "Folsom Prison Blues" are more universal. Cash never shook the lingering feelings of guilt he carried about Jack's death. And the damage he did to himself and loved ones during his years of addiction wracked his conscience—a sadness about the past that would eventually find expression late in his life in his cover of "Hurt" by Nine Inch Nails. Our prisons are often emotional and spiritual, with walls built high using bricks of guilt and regret. As Cash observed, "I think prison songs are popular because most of us are living in one little kind of prison or another, and whether we know it or not the words of a song about someone who is actually in prison speak for a lot of us who might appear not to be, but really are."[6]

Free or incarcerated, we've all experienced the alienation of "Folsom Prison Blues." Prisoners of guilt, shame, loss, and regret, we observe the happy lives of others carrying on cheerfully. Spiritually, we hear the cell door slam, and we listen to the lonesome whistle pass and fade into the distance. People are traveling on to happiness and fulfillment, and we are left behind.

Artistically, 1968 would prove to be a pivotal year in the career of Johnny Cash. He'd left Sun and joined Columbia ten years earlier, and both Columbia and Cash were happy with the arrangement: Columbia because Cash was selling records, and Cash because Columbia gave him more artistic freedom, allowing him to record gospel music and his concept albums. But by 1968, executives at Columbia were growing worried. Although Cash was still selling records (the smash hit "Ring of Fire" had recently buoyed him), Cash's appeal was waning, and his audience was aging. Artists like the Beach Boys and the Beatles had the ear of the younger generation. *Pet Sounds* came out in 1966, and *Sgt. Pepper* a year later. It was the Age of Aquarius and the Summer of Love. Young people weren't listening to country music.

Cash searched for his voice and vision, but he was also looking for something more meaningful and personal. As I'll describe later, 1968 was a pivotal year in Cash's personal life. After a decade of heavy drug use, Cash sobered up. The year before, during which he and Vivian divorced, had been the darkest year of his life, a personal hell. But rising up from the grave, Cash experienced a series of profound spiritual transformations. So on the stage of Folsom Prison in 1968, Cash wasn't just trying to sell more records; he was looking for redemption.

Cash knew what he needed to do. Wanting to capture the electricity of his performances behind prison walls, performances until then hidden from public view, Cash pitched the idea of a live prison concert to the Columbia execs. They weren't impressed and shot the idea down. Absolutely, there would be no recordings of live prison concerts.

So Cash and his new producer, Bob Johnson, did the obvious thing. They ignored the execs and went ahead anyway.

Looking to book the concert, Johnson first rang up San Quentin. There was no answer. He called Folsom next. The warden picked up and said, yes, he'd love to have Cash come play another concert. Perfect. The date was set for January 13, 1968.

The day of the Folsom concert dawned dreary, overcast, and gray. Somber skies matched somber moods. Cash and his large entourage seemed uncharacteristically quiet and reflective, as if they sensed the importance of that moment in their lives. Cash especially faced a fork in the road, and he had questions about whether he was going to be able to meet the moment.

The prison itself was tense that day. Two weeks before, two inmates had attacked a guard, gagged him, and held him at knifepoint. A few weeks after the concert, as a part of an inmate protest, a work stoppage jolted Folsom. Cash's performance would prove to be an oasis of light in a dark and stormy place.

The mood began to lighten as the band relaxed in a makeshift dressing room off the prison kitchen. Around 9:40 a.m., about a thousand prisoners began making their way to dining room number two, where a stage had been constructed and festooned with the words "Welcome Johnny Cash."

Two shows were scheduled for the day, one in the morning and one in the afternoon. Johnson wanted the second show as insurance, in case something went wrong with the equipment, the audience, or the performance during the morning. In the end, however, almost the entirety of the final album came from the morning concert.

Once the inmates were seated, disc jockey Hugh Cherry took the stage as the concert emcee, informing the audience that the concert was being recorded. Carl Perkins, a dear friend of Cash's who regularly toured with him, emerged next onstage to rip through his signature song, "Blue Suede Shoes," the song Elvis had covered and made famous. After Perkins, the Statler Brothers, who also toured with Cash, sang "This Old House." With the audience primed and ready, the time had arrived for the main act. Cherry reappeared onstage to prepare and quiet the audience.

In the hushed silence, Cash walked up to the microphone and uttered his iconic introduction: "Hello, I'm Johnny Cash."

And the room erupted.

Whenever I hear that moment, it still gives me chills. It's one of the greatest moments in music history. There's been nothing like it, before or since.

The concert itself was, by turns, shocking, hilarious, inspirational, and disturbing. Cash didn't avoid the darkness of Folsom; he embraced and thrilled to it. You wince at a joke song about an execution ("25 Minutes to Go") and experience despair as Cash sings about an inmate committing suicide ("The Wall"). And then there's the sociopathic romp "Cocaine Blues," a song about a domestic homicide sung by Cash with such glee it makes you wonder if Cash wasn't pushing the solidarity thing a bit too far. And then at the end, out of nowhere, Jesus shows up with the closing song, "Greystone Chapel."

At Folsom Prison has it all—trains, Jesus, and murder.

At *Folsom Prison* went on to establish itself as one of the greatest albums of all time, becoming the quintessential expression of Cash's Man in Black solidarity with the forgotten, the discarded, and the oppressed. The album spoke in a way no artist was speaking at the time, and this at the height of the protest-minded, justice-oriented, socially conscious 1960s. Michael Streissguth makes the contrast:

> *Folsom* was also a social statement on behalf of disenfranchised people, as potent as any such statement in the roiling 1960s, for by appearing in front of America's modern-day lepers and recording and releasing what came of it, [Cash] unapologetically told his listeners that these locked-away men deserved the compassion, if not the liberation, that the 1960s offered. He used his art as a battering ram to smash through conventional notions of prisoners and prisons. None of Cash's peers in popular music ever dared to so brazenly wield their music, not Dylan, not Zappa, not the Beatles, not Country Joe McDonald, not Crosby, Stills, Nash, and (or) Young, not any big-selling artist who composed and performed so-called protest music in the 1960s. Transcending the decade of its birth, the album still resonates in the early 21st century, when criminal justice remains anything but rational and man has never appeared more insensitive to his fellow man.[7]

The socially enlightened bards of the sixties loved to wax poetic about love and justice. "All you need is love," crooned the Beatles.

John Lennon held a "sleep-in," considered by many to be a provocative statement for peace. Johnny Cash, by contrast, performed in un-air-conditioned maximum-security prisons on makeshift stages, dozens of times for no money. *Sgt. Pepper* and *Pet Sounds* are regularly ranked as the number-one and number-two greatest albums of all time. But if hope is where your ass is, they don't hold a candle to *At Folsom Prison*. Words are nice, and so are songs, but when it comes to justice and love, it's where you put your ass that ultimately matters.

But beyond solidarity and justice, there is a deeper spiritual insight about *At Folsom Prison*. The thunderous reception received that day—and all the cheering, applause, hollering, laughing, and calling out on the album—reveals a truth: the star of the show that day wasn't Johnny Cash. The real stars of *At Folsom Prison*—and this is what has made the album so singular and iconic—were the prisoners in the audience. Both Cash and Johnson knew that would be the case, which is why they were so passionate about recording a live prison concert. They knew if they could get the sound of those men on tape, they would have something unforgettable. And they were right. Those were the sounds that captured my attention and heart as I drove out to my Bible study on that Monday night when I first listened to the album.

And what that means, in a very real way, is that the inmates of Folsom Prison saved Johnny Cash. In 1968, Cash stood at a perilous crossroads, musically and personally. His career was on the downswing. His recent sobriety and spiritual awakening were shaky and fragile; in fact, Cash had even popped a few pills to deal with his nerves that day on the stage of Folsom.

All that to say, if the Folsom concert hadn't gone well, Cash's life could have turned out very differently, probably tragically. Cash went to Folsom looking for grace. And salvation came to him that day in the embrace of thieves, outlaws, and murderers.

This reversal teases us throughout the Bible—how God comes to us in unlikely people. In the words of the book of Hebrews, we entertain angels unawares. In Matthew 25, Jesus tells the parable of the sheep and the goats. On the day of judgment, God separates the sheep and the goats, the saved and the damned. Welcoming the sheep into heaven, the Lord says, "Come, you who are blessed by my Father. For I was hungry and you gave me something to eat, I was thirsty and you gave me something to drink, I was a stranger and you invited me in, I needed clothes and you clothed me, I was sick and you looked after me, I was in prison and you came to visit me." But the sheep are confused by this declaration and ask, "Lord, when did we see you hungry and feed you, or thirsty and give you something to drink? When did we see you a stranger and invite you in, or needing clothes and clothe you? When did we see you sick or in prison and go to visit you?" And the Lord responds, "Truly I tell you, whatever you did for one of the least of these brothers and sisters of mine, you did for me."

Notice the reversal, one so very hard for us to wrap our heads around. In the story, Jesus isn't identified as the *sheep*, the do-gooder who is visiting the prisoner, clothing the naked, and sheltering the homeless. Jesus comes to us in the parable as the homeless and the prisoner. We visit prisoners and shelter the homeless not to be like Jesus but to welcome Jesus. When we welcome the homeless and the incarcerated, we aren't the saviors—*we are the ones being saved.*[8]

That's exactly what happened to Johnny Cash at Folsom Prison in 1968. He came looking for redemption, and he was saved by the prisoners. Cash found salvation among the lost. He found Jesus among the damned.

This is also my story, and it's the reason I was so powerfully affected by *At Folsom Prison*. I started teaching the Bible class out at the maximum-security French Robertson Unit because my faith was struggling. I was spiritually dry and looking for God. And the first place to look for God is in hell, right? So I started driving out to the prison, hoping that Jesus would show up as he promised in Matthew 25. Whenever we visit the prisoner, Jesus said, we visit him. I was desperately seeking Jesus, and he had told me where to look.

I found Jesus in the prison. What happened to Johnny Cash happened to me, too: the incarcerated saved me. Week after week for me, it's similar to what you hear on *At Folsom Prison*. Grace comes to me in the outpouring of gratitude the Men in White give me. The love they share is both humbling and life-giving.

On Sundays, I go to a wonderful church, the Highland Church of Christ, but my real worship experience, the spiritual highlight of my week, occurs during those Monday-night old-time, tent-revival, gospel hymn sings we have, using the same songs that sustained Johnny Cash as his favorite form of prayer. These hours of singing in the prison have been my manna, sustaining me week after week.

This is why, after my first listen to *At Folsom Prison*, I could not get enough Johnny Cash. In his music, I found someone who had heard what I had heard, who had seen what I had seen, who had experienced what I had experienced, and whose life had been changed as my life had been changed.

I listened to *At Folsom Prison* as if it were a tent-revival testimony. For I, too, had been saved by the damned.

CHAPTER 5

"GREYSTONE CHAPEL"

I'd like to take a knife . . . and just cut you all to hell," Glen Sherley said coldly to Marshall Grant. "It's not because I don't love you, because I do. But that's just the type of person I am. I'd rather kill you than talk to you."[1] Sherley was touring and performing with Johnny Cash at the time. Disturbed by Sherley's murderous confession, Grant told Cash that he had to do something. Cash sat down with Sherley and informed him he was off the tour.

It was a crushing moment. Having Sherley onstage had been proof of everything Cash had been advocating for by way of prison reform. Sherley had become famous as the Folsom inmate who wrote "Greystone Chapel" on *At Folsom Prison*. Seated next to Cash, Sherley had even testified before Congress that he was evidence that the incarcerated could be rehabilitated and should be treated with compassion.

Cash had helped Sherley get out of prison, giving the ex-con a new beginning. But the redemption story never materialized. On May 11, 1978, Glen Sherley shot himself in the head.

Rehearsing before concerts was a rare thing for Johnny Cash. So when he called for a rehearsal before the Folsom concert, everyone knew how important this show was for Johnny. Gathered in a banquet room at the El Rancho Inn in Sacramento, the band worked through the set list. Many of the expected standards were there: "I Walk the Line," "Give My Love to Rose," "I Still Miss Someone," and, of course, "Folsom Prison Blues." But the band spent most of the rehearsal time working on a new song, "Greystone Chapel."

Accounts differ about when Cash first came across "Greystone Chapel." The most dramatic version of the story is that Cash got the song the evening before the concert and made an inspired, last-minute decision to add it to the show. What we do know is that Floyd Gressett gave a tape of "Greystone Chapel" to Cash at some point before the concert, perhaps as early as a year before. Taken with the idea of performing a song written by a convict doing time at Folsom, Cash wanted the song in the Folsom show.

A pastor and close friend of Cash's, Floyd Gressett walked alongside Cash during some of the darkest days of his addiction. And when Cash started turning back to God in the late sixties, he began attending Gressett's nondenominational church, the first time Cash had regularly attended church since his childhood in Arkansas. Gressett visited and did pastoral work at Folsom, and he had helped Cash schedule the first concert at the prison. Knowing of their close relationship, Sherley asked Gressett to pass his tape of "Greystone Chapel" on to Cash.

The greystone chapel of the song is a physical description of the chapel on the grounds at Folsom. In Sherley's song, the physical presence of the building functions as a metaphor for the vibrant spirituality that pulses through the prison, in spite of the surrounding ridicule and disbelief. Cash loved the imagery and felt it would be the perfect spiritual note on which to conclude the show. As Michael Streissguth observes, "An anthem for the imprisoned, 'Greystone Chapel' describes the mind that with Christ had transcended its cell. . . . It promised to be the perfect climax in the drama Cash planned to stage, a message of redemption dispatched by the very criminal mind he'd be entertaining."[2]

Rehearsing at the El Rancho the night before, Cash and the band worked on an arrangement for the song. Carl Perkins would open up the song with a country swing lick. June Carter and the Statler Brothers worked out the harmonies.

The next day, late in the show, the time for "Greystone Chapel" arrived. "This next song was written by a man right here in Folsom Prison, and last night was the first time I've ever sung this song," Cash announced to the audience. "We may be a little rough on it today. . . . Anyway, this song was written by our friend Glen Sherley." Cash looked down at Sherley, who was seated in the rows at the foot of the stage. "Hope we do your song justice, Glen."[3]

Cash looked at his band and confirmed the key of the song, and then Carl Perkins started in. Upon hearing the first line referencing their very own Folsom chapel, the crowd erupted. Streissguth describes the response from the inmates: "When Cash uttered these [opening] lines, the applause cracked up from the floor like unexpected thunder. Throughout the show the reaction had not been so decisive, so serious. But somehow 'Greystone' commented on their plight like no other song that day had, not even 'Folsom Prison Blues.' It was a symbol of Cash's bond with convicts and the possibility of redemption."[4]

When the song ended, applause rained down again. Cash leaned over and shook Glen Sherley's hand from the stage.

———

That moment during the Folsom concert, choosing to sing a song written by a Folsom inmate, may be one of the most iconic examples of Johnny Cash's "Man in Black" solidarity. And for a season, the story seemed to get even better. After the morning show, Reverend Gressett introduced Cash to Sherley. The two chatted for a few minutes. Cash learned that Sherley was in Folsom for armed robbery, that he'd written many other songs in addition to "Greystone Chapel," and that Sherley had a five-year-to-life sentence. Cash promised to keep in touch and left with the resolution to help get Sherley parole if he could.

Cash followed through. He spent months lobbying on Sherley's behalf, asking the California prison authorities to grant Sherley parole. He pulled his strings, asking the Rev. Billy Graham to call Governor Ronald Reagan on Sherley's behalf. Cash even promised the parole authorities that he would provide Sherley a job if released.

All of the advocacy paid off. On March 8, 1971, Sherley was granted parole. Cash announced to the press that Sherley would be joining his tour and signing a contract with his music-publishing company. When Sherley stepped out of the prison, Cash was there, waiting to drive him home.

———

Many of those close to Cash, however, harbored doubts about Glen Sherley. After all, Cash had spent only a few minutes talking to Sherley after the Folsom concert. He hardly knew the man he was vouching for. Marshall Grant, for one, felt that Sherley was using Cash. "His plan was to see if he could make a mark somehow with John, and maybe somehow someway get out," shared Grant. "Glen told me this himself."[5]

Things started off well. Sherley released a self-titled album that appeared on the *Billboard* country charts. He appeared with Cash before a Senate committee looking into prison reform, sharing with Congress, "I was a three-time loser when John reached out his hand to me in 1968, and since then I sincerely believe that I have become a worthwhile person and can contribute to society outside as well as contributing to society inside."[6]

But problems soon began to surface. In person, Sherley wasn't a very productive or effective songwriter, leading many in Cash's circle to wonder if he really was the one who had written "Greystone Chapel." (They suspected another Folsom inmate, Harlen Sanders, had written the songs Sherley took credit for.) On the road, Sherley slept during the day and stayed up all night, interfering with his ability to keep up with the demanding tour schedule. Eventually, tensions got to the point where Sherley made his menacing comment to Grant: "I'd like to take a knife . . . and just cut you all to hell."

Kicked off the tour, Sherley drifted. He divorced the woman he had married right after his parole. He resumed his drug habit. He started living out of his truck. And then, on May 11, 1978, he committed suicide.

———

The tragedy of Glen Sherley illustrates the cost and the heartache of solidarity. We romanticize solidarity, even in the life of Johnny Cash. I myself am tempted to do so in this very book. But that iconic moment of solidarity in *At Folsom Prison*, Johnny Cash singing "Greystone Chapel," has a tragic ending. In the end, Johnny Cash couldn't save Glen Sherley. As Rosanne Cash observed about her father's relationship with Glen Sherley and others he tried to help, "You can't hasten someone else's recovery or enlightenment. I think my dad had a sense of maybe he could and it didn't turn out well all the time."[7] We should remind ourselves of these sad outcomes whenever we talk about solidarity in the life of Johnny Cash.

Our trouble is this: We want solidarity and salvation to be the same thing. But they're not.

First of all, when we confuse solidarity with salvation, we tend to objectify others. Whenever we see ourselves as saving people, we make ourselves the hero of the story, a moral drama in which we're riding in on a white horse. In that story, the people we so nobly rescue are just moral props, passive recipients of our kindness and generosity. Aren't they lucky that we showed up? A lot of compassionate people fall into this trap, failing to see how our desire to save others can be both selfish and dehumanizing.

Solidarity is different from salvation. Solidarity doesn't presume we have the answers or the ability to save anyone. Solidarity makes us available to others, but it recognizes other's competencies, seeing people as possessing the resources to help themselves if we'd just get out of the way. That's not to say we're useless, just that we don't dictate what, how, or if we can be useful. When we're trying to save people, we're talking and giving directions. With solidarity, we're listening and receiving directions. We're not the heroes of the story; we bear witness to the heroism of others. In solidarity, we are the ones being saved.

The currency of solidarity isn't moral heroism—rescuing, fixing, and saving people. The currency of solidarity is relationship, mutuality, and friendship. And if that's the case, we come face-to-face with the reality that relationships are risky and that we can't guarantee the outcomes, no matter how hard we try. We aren't in control, and some stories end sadly and tragically.

Sometimes we try to save people as a defense mechanism, as a way to deny the risk and avoid the potential hurt. We keep trying to save people because to admit failure is to come face-to-face with loss. And fearing the pain of that loss, we refuse to give up, churning and churning away, fretting and worrying, trying to rescue someone, especially a person we dearly love. We don't want to face the pain, so we keep trying to save them.

I'm not trying to give an apology for resignation, nor am I giving permission to give up on people. I'm just pointing out that our messiah complexes are often strategies for delaying and avoiding grief. And if we're not careful, this can lead to burnout and despair. In trying to save the world, we'll either exhaust ourselves or fall into depression—often both at the same time.

Try as we might, some stories don't end well. Glen Sherley's didn't. There is risk in relationship. We don't always get the "happily ever after." Solidarity comes with an emotional price tag. So if you invest in the lives of others, there are going to be seasons of pain and loss. Wanting to avoid this, we opt for either apathy or the moral heroism of riding in on a white horse. Apathy keeps you numb, and the white horse makes you feel in control. Either way, it's a strategy for avoiding heartbreak.

Solidarity is the more difficult, more painful path.

———

So where's the good news in any of this? Where's the gospel according to Johnny Cash in the story of Glen Sherley?

I was counseling a friend recently. She was walking the path of solidarity with someone who was making self-destructive and unhealthy choices. So much love, time, energy, and money had been poured into this person, for years and years, but nothing had changed; my friend was reaching her limit. The hope of salvation was coming to an end, and the shadow of grief and loss was finally closing in. Should she finally let this person go?

Of course, I couldn't give her an answer. No one can. And we all make different choices here. Tearfully and with hearts breaking, some of us do cut the string. We draw the line. Some of us can't do that, choosing to fight until the bitter end, no matter the cost to our bank accounts or mental health. And no one can stand in judgment of either of these choices. We make them for reasons uniquely our own.

But this is what I did say to my friend: "The economy of love is paid in tears. Sooner or later, grief is the price we will pay for loving someone deeply and well. There is a price to love." So I told my friend, "I don't know the right choice; I can't tell you what to do. But I can tell you this much. If you get to the grief, you've loved a person well. Most people don't ever get to the tears. They've given up long ago. But you," I told my friend, "you've loved a person deep into the pain. So the sadness, while hard, is holy ground. Our tears are sacraments, visible signs of the invisible grace of a loved poured out."

A tragic story hovers behind "Greystone Chapel." I think of that sadness whenever I see the iconic picture of Johnny Cash shaking Glen Sherley's hand from the stage at Folsom prison. Solidarity can end with heartbreak. And if there is any good news to the sadness, it is this: you know you've loved a person well when you make it to the tears.

After Glen Sherley died, Johnny Cash paid for the funeral expenses.

CHAPTER 6

"SAN QUENTIN"

Sing it, Cash!" the prisoners roared and screamed. "You know it man, we're all in hell in here!"[1]

My favorite Johnny Cash moment, which comes from his second live prison album, is the moment when Johnny Cash almost started a prison riot. After the critical and commercial success of *At Folsom Prison*, both Cash and Columbia Records wanted to keep riding the wave of enthusiasm and interest. A follow-up concert was quickly scheduled for another infamous California prison, where the state's Death Row was located. In 1969, just a year after the Folsom concert, *At San Quentin* was released.

Now, if you look at the track listing of the songs on *At San Quentin*, you will notice something curious. The song "San Quentin" is listed twice, back to back. That's not an error. The reason the song was played twice was, by all accounts, a potentially dangerous moment. And as someone who spends a lot of time working in a prison, I consider it my favorite illustration of the gospel according to Johnny Cash.

Upon its release, *At San Quentin* quickly joined *At Folsom Prison* as one of Cash's best-selling albums. In the eyes of music historians and critics, *At Folsom Prison* is considered Cash's greatest album. But among Cash fans, *At San Quentin* may be more beloved and popular, due to the iconic hit single from that album, a song that is adored by Cash fans and would go on to become his biggest-selling single: "A Boy Named Sue."

Cash didn't write "A Boy Named Sue," and the song almost didn't make it into the concert. The song was written by Shel Silverstein, author of the beloved children's book *The Giving Tree*. Along with being a famous cartoonist and children's book author, Silverstein also had a music career as a songwriter and performer. He released his recording of "A Boy Named Sue" on his own album *Boy Named Sue and His Other Country Songs*.

Cash was told about Silverstein's quirky song by Don Davis, a music producer and family friend (Davis was married to Anita Carter, sister of June Carter Cash). Cash did have a soft spot for goofy songs. In 1966, he'd released a whole album of humorous novelty songs, entitled *Everybody Loves a Nut*. Davis felt "A Boy Named Sue" would make a great song for the upcoming San Quentin concert, since Cash had had success at Folsom with another Silverstein song, "25 Minutes to Go."

But Cash didn't plan to perform "A Boy Named Sue" at San Quentin. He liked the song but left it behind to record when he got back home. As he and June packed for the trip, it was June who threw the song lyrics onto a stack of material Cash was taking to California.

During the concert rehearsals, Cash found the lyrics and brought them to the show. Toward the end of the concert, when Cash felt they had recorded enough material for an album, he pulled out the song and asked the band to make up some music. Tentative at first, the musicians fell into a groove, and Cash recorded, live and unrehearsed, the only song of his that made it into the top ten of the Billboard Hot 100 chart. "A Boy Named Sue" spent three weeks as the number-two most popular song in the nation, bested only by the Rolling Stones' "Honky Tonk Women."

If "A Boy Named Sue" was improvised at the last minute, the song Cash really had prepared for the concert was "San Quentin." Midway through the concert, Cash stepped up to the microphone and shifted into a personal, serious tone. "I was thinking about you guys yesterday," he started. "I've been here three times before, and I think I understand a little bit how you feel about some things." The room quieted while the audience listened. "It's none of my business how you feel about some other things," Cash continued, "and I don't give a damn about how you feel about some other things. But anyway, I tried to put myself in your place, and I believe this is the way that I would feel about San Quentin."[2]

The song began with some heavy guitar notes, and then Cash spat out a venomous opening line describing San Quentin as a living hell. Hearing that, the room erupted. For two minutes, the song continued in that vein, a sustained prophetic rebuke of San Quentin and the entire criminal justice system. Cheers erupted throughout the entire song, carrying Cash to his final, biting lines:

San Quentin, may you rot and burn in hell.
May your walls fall down and may I live to tell.
May all the world forget you ever stood.
And the world regret you did no good.

"San Quentin" is a raw, harsh indictment of the prison-industrial complex, a litany recounting its inhumanity, brutality, and ineffectiveness. With the song, Cash tapped into the heart and soul of the San Quentin inmates. He channeled their rage and despair. Cash had, in that moment, become one of them.

When the song ended, the applause was thunderous and sustained. The prisoners called out to Cash, insisting that he sing the song again. And so he did.

When Cash spat out the final, biting lines of the song for a second time, the room exploded again, even louder than the first time. Breaking the rules, inmates stood on the tables to cheer and scream. An ominous, dangerous energy filled the room. Men began shouting out, "You give us the word, Cash, and we'll beat the hell out of them, just for the hell of it!"[3]

"All the guards were nervous," recounted Bob Johnson, Cash's producer. "They thought there was going to be a riot." Cash sensed the danger, how his song of solidarity had pushed the room to a tipping point. "He realized that all he had to say was 'Let's go!' and there would have been a full-scale riot," Johnson continued, "He told me after, 'I was tempted.'"[4]

If you really want to understand what made Johnny Cash so special as an artist and human being, take a minute to listen to the reaction on the album after the second playing of "San Quentin."

—

The reason I love this moment is why the room got so close to exploding. It was all about solidarity—Johnny Cash being the Man in Black. In the song, Cash had attempted to see San Quentin as the men in the audience saw San Quentin. And Cash was so successful in portraying their world, expressing the feelings they were feeling, that a spark was ignited. The response from the San Quentin prisoners that day is, perhaps, the single best illustration of Johnny Cash's ability to express solidarity with the broken and the lost. Listen to it: the roar after the second singing of "San Quentin" is the sound of the gospel according to Johnny Cash.

The pain, anger, and despair of the song "San Quentin" illustrate how expressions of solidarity can be harsh and bleak. Too often, the church sweeps past the suffering and sorrow of the world to get to the good news and the happy-ever-after ending. But the gospel doesn't take shortcuts. Yes, there's resurrection—but the cross came first. We get to the good news of Easter Sunday only after crying out, "My God, my God, why have you forsaken me?"

If "San Quentin" is anything, it's a lament. And lament is something Christians, especially American Christians, don't do very well. In our relationship with God, we tend to privilege certainty over doubt, praise over lament, and positivity over negativity. American

Christianity works with a bipolar model regarding the relationship between faith and lament. We assume that faith and lament are on opposite ends of the same continuum. When you have faith, you don't lament—you don't ever doubt, question, or express anger toward God. Conversely, if you express lament, if you doubt or question God, you're seen as lacking in faith. Faith and lament are considered antithetical. As faith goes up, lament goes down, and vice versa. Lament is a faith problem, it's assumed.

The church routinely fails to consider how lament can coexist with a mature, vibrant faith. We miss the fact that lament is actually an *expression* of a mature, vibrant faith. Lament isn't the opposite of faith; rather, faith gives birth to lament. Questioning and crying out to God are a deep, honest manifestation of faith.

Our avoidance of lament is puzzling, given how the Bible is full of examples of faith and doubt existing side by side. For example, the majority of the Psalms are laments. Worship for the people of God is frequently an expression of lament. Think also of Job, how his faith was expressed in the anguish and accusations he hurled at God. And then there is Jesus himself, crying out and questioning from the cross, "My God, my God, why have you forsaken me?" For a moment, even God doubted.

The Old Testament scholar Walter Brueggemann classifies the psalms as songs of either "orientation" or "disorientation." Psalms of orientation are songs of praise, confidence, and trust in God. The world is morally coherent in psalms of orientation: the righteous are getting rewarded and the wicked are getting punished (see Psalm 1 as an example). Psalms of disorientation, by contrast, are songs of lament, grief, and protest. In psalms of disorientation, the world is spinning out of control, good people are suffering, and God seems absent and unconcerned. Again, while most of the psalms are songs of disorientation, the church tends to avoid singing these songs on Sunday mornings, even when the world seems to be spinning out of control. This avoidance of lament in the face of our pain is perplexing, and Brueggemann gives his assessment about why churches tend to avoid these psalms in their worship services, and encourages people of faith to sing them more:

> I think that serious religious use of the lament psalms has been minimal because we have believed that faith does not mean to acknowledge and embrace negativity. We have thought that acknowledgment of negativity was somehow an act of unfaith, as though the very speech about it conceded too much about God's "loss of control."
>
> The point to be urged here is this: The use of these "psalms of darkness" may be judged by the world to be *acts of unfaith and failure*, but for the trusting community, their use is *an act of bold faith*.[5]

Lament isn't a failure or lack of faith. Lament is an act of bold, trusting faith in the midst of pain, suffering, and confusion. In fact, if we ignore lament, if we avoid giving voice to despair and rage, the gospel loses its ability to speak honestly, realistically, and truthfully. Without lament, faith grows naïve and superficial—a happy, fake, glossy façade we paint over the pain and confusion. In addition, lament is the cry of the oppressed, a song of resistance. When we avoid lament, we are marginalizing the voices crying out in pain around the world.

In sum, lament is the shadow of the gospel, the moon to the gospel's sun. The bright hope of the gospel creates sharp, dark outlines of contrast around all that is unjust and broken. Lament is that gap separating the new heavens and the new earth from the shattered world we find around us. In pointing toward that gap, we are not failing or denying the gospel; instead, we are praying with tears and raw, cracked voices, "May your kingdom come, on earth as it is in heaven."

The rage and despair of "San Quentin" might not sound like a gospel hymn, but sung by those aching for the redemption and reconciliation of all things, the song is an anthem of resistance and hope.

The sound of the gospel isn't always nice and sweet, and it's often found in some surprising, unsettling places. Just listen to the roar of San Quentin.

CHAPTER 7

"THE BALLAD OF IRA HAYES"

DJs—station managers—owners, etc., where are your *guts?*"
Readers of *Billboard* magazine in August 1964 were treated to a full-page advertisement, taken out and paid for by Johnny Cash, calling out radio stations across the country for their lack of moral courage. The song at the heart of the dispute was Cash's cover of Peter La Farge's "The Ballad of Ira Hayes," the first single from Cash's recently released album of Native American protest songs, *Bitter Tears*. Billboard declined to give much attention to *Bitter Tears*, and DJs across the country weren't playing "The Ballad of Ira Hayes." Livid, Cash in his full-page ad called out what he felt was the problem: "'Ballad of Ira Hayes' *is* strong medicine. So is Rochester—Harlem—Birmingham and Vietnam."

The Beatles were topping the charts in 1964 with "I Want to Hold Your Hand," and the Beach Boys with "I Get Around." Johnny Cash, by contrast, was fighting to get airplay for an album of protest songs highlighting the plight of indigenous peoples at the hands of the American empire. As the liner notes of *Bitter Tears* read, "Hear the words [of this album] well and you will discover that simply because we are white, that does not make us pure."

That was not a greatest plug to sell some records. No wonder the album wasn't getting much airplay. But outside of *At Folsom Prison*, no album better illustrates Cash's solidarity with the oppressed than *Bitter Tears*. As Native American activist Dennis Banks remarked about the album, "To me, Cash's album is one of the earliest and most significant statements on behalf of Native people and our issues."[1]

———

Captain Ira Hayes of the United States Marine Corps was a hero of World War II. When he returned from duty in the Pacific, the military paraded him around the country. He shook the hand of the president and had the New York Stock Exchange stop trading to unfurl a banner that read, "Welcome Iwo Jima Heroes."

Ten years later, one month shy of the moment in history that had made him famous, the lifeless, frozen body of Ira Hayes was found lying next to a rusted-out truck on the Gila River Indian Reservation in Sacaton, Arizona. Captain Hayes died of exposure to the elements and overconsumption of alcohol. He was thirty-two years old.

Ira Hayes was a member of the Akimel O'otham people, called the Pima ("River People") by the Spanish, due to their agricultural skills in creating irrigation systems throughout the Gila River Valley in what is today Arizona. A quiet and humble people, the Pima cultivated their crops of corn, beans, and squash for over two millennia before the westward expansion of white settlers displaced them.

Ira Hayes was born on the Gila River Reservation on January 12, 1923. In 1942, a year after the attack on Pearl Harbor, the nineteen-year-old Hayes joined the Marine Corps, hoping to bring honor to his tribe and perhaps change the way Native peoples were viewed and treated in America. Three years after joining the Marines, he found himself in the middle of the hellscape known as Iwo Jima.

While only eight square miles in size, Iwo Jima was strategically important to the American war effort, because taking the small island would deprive the Japanese of tactically significant airfields. Just 760 miles from Tokyo, Iwo Jima also would be strategically useful if the United States had to conduct an invasion of mainland Japan.

Prior to the Marines' invasion of the island, about twenty-one thousand Japanese troops dug in, creating a network of tunnels, pillboxes, and bunkers throughout the island. So entrenched and difficult to displace were the Japanese defenders, who had vowed to fight to the death, Iwo Jima became one of the fiercest and bloodiest battles in World War II. Of the Japanese troops defending Iwo Jima, only 216 were taken prisoner alive.

The Marines invaded Iwo Jima on February 19, 1945. After days of fierce combat, most of the island was subdued, leaving one final objective: taking and securing Mount Suribachi, the highest point on the island. The Americans knew that Mount Suribachi was a honeycomb of underground tunnels connecting the mountain to other parts of the island. After a small patrol reconnoitered all the way to the top of Suribachi (most of the Japanese defenders remained in their underground tunnels), a platoon of Marines from E Company were sent up to take the mountain and to raise the American flag at the summit if they were successful. E Company succeeded, and they raised the flag.

E Company's flag raising on Mount Suribachi—known as the "first flag raising" of Iwo Jima—was the first time an American flag was raised on Japanese territory. Recognizing the significance of the flag, Secretary of the Navy James Forrestal, who had landed on the island in time to see its raising, wanted the Marines to bring the flag back and replace it with another one. Four Marines were chosen by Rene Gagnon to go up and replace the flag on the summit of Suribachi: Franklin Sousley, Harlon Block, Mike Strank, and Ira Hayes.

The men struggled back up the mountain, laying a telephone wire as they climbed, watchful for any Japanese who might jump out from a crack in the rocks. The group eventually arrived at the summit and began to lift a heavy drainage pipe to serve as a flagpole. Seeing the men struggle to lift the pole, John Bradley jumped in to lend a hand. Photographer Joe Rosenthal was close by and snapped a picture of the men attaching the flag to the pole. The photo Rosenthal took, "Raising the Flag on Iwo Jima," electrified the United States, pumping life into the war effort, and the photo has become one of the most famous and iconic pictures in American history. No one cared that this was the *second* flag, the *replacement* flag, raised on Iwo Jima. The men in the photo, the Native American Ira Hayes among them, were instant war heroes.

Tragically, only three of the men in the photograph survived Iwo Jima: Ira Hayes, Rene Gagnon, and John Bradley, who lost a leg. Upon their return home, the men toured around the country in an effort to raise war bonds. The constant media attention and the accolades wore on Hayes, especially when he met the family members of dead soldiers. He began to drink, and he was removed from the war bond tour. Hayes returned to the reservation, haunted by the war. He continued to drink, and over the years, he slipped deeper into a despondency and despair that never left him. On the morning of January 24, 1955, Ira Hayes's body was discovered outside, frozen in the cold after a night of heavy drinking.

The tragic story of Ira Hayes captured the imagination of folk singer Peter La Farge, who wrote the song "The Ballad of Ira Hayes" and recorded it in 1960. The song recounts the entire sad tale—how the Pima people, skilled and proud agriculturalists, had their water and land stolen from them; how Hayes signed up to go war; how he raised the flag, survived the battle of Iwo Jima, and returned a war hero; and how he started drinking and died alone in a ditch. The song uses the story of Ira Hayes to indict America's exploitation of Native peoples, as evidenced by the dried-up waters of the Gila River and the indifference toward the trauma of a damaged war hero:

Then Ira started drinking hard,
jail was often his home.
They let him raise the flag and lower it,
like you'd throw a dog a bone.
He died drunk early one morning,
alone in the land he fought to save.
Two inches of water and a lonely ditch,
was a grave for Ira Hayes.

In the mid-1960s, Johnny Cash was making connections with the exploding folk scene and its activist participation in the civil rights movement and, later, the anti–Vietnam War protests. Pete Seeger and

Woody Guthrie were all the rage, and newcomers like Joan Baez and Bob Dylan were starting to make a splash. Because of his early years with Sun Records, Cash was often associated with early rock 'n' roll. But Cash saw himself as a storyteller in the folk music tradition. The deep musical influence of the Carter Family on Cash's music, to say nothing of his marriage into the Carter family, speak to Cash's roots in folk music, so it was natural that Cash would be drawn to the emerging folk artists. In 1964, the year *Bitter Tears* was released, Cash electrified the folk scene with his performance at the Newport Folk Festival. Though he might have started as a rockabilly star, at Newport Cash felt he was among his people. And the centerpiece of Cash's Newport set list, which included old standards like "I Walk the Line," was his cover of La Farge's "The Ballad of Ira Hayes."

Cash had met La Farge a few years earlier, and the "The Ballad of Ira Hayes" fired both his imagination and his heart for the underdog. For many years, Cash had been dismayed by the plight of Native Americans. The issues were front-page news in the early and midsixties with the building of the Kinzua Dam in Pennsylvania, a federal project to control the flooding of the Allegheny River. The lake that would be created by the dam, the Allegheny Reservoir, was going to displace about six hundred Seneca from ten thousand acres of land they occupied under the 1794 Treaty of Canandaigua. The Seneca appealed to President Kennedy to stop the construction of the dam. Kennedy denied the request, marking yet another treaty broken by the American government. The Seneca were removed, and the dam was built in 1965.

Cash also covered Peter La Farge's song about the Kinzua Dam, "As Long as the Grass Shall Grow," on *Bitter Tears*. The song recounts how treaty after treaty had been broken by the American government, starting with George Washington all the way to Kennedy. During the years of the Kinzua Dam dispute, Cash participated in benefit concerts to help stop the construction. For his efforts, the Seneca gave Cash the name Ha-Gao-Ta, meaning Storyteller.

The story of Ira Hayes and the building of the Kinzua Dam so captured Cash's attention and imagination that he decided to do a concept album devoted to the Native American experience—*Bitter Tears,* a prophetic wakeup call. Preparing for the album, Cash visited the mother of Ira Hayes. During the visit, Nancy Hayes gave Cash an "Apache tear," one of the black obsidian stones found in the American Southwest.

The legend behind the Apache tear goes like this: A band of Apache warriors were trapped by the US Cavalry on a cliff. Rather than surrender, the warriors rode their horses over the cliff to their death. The Apache women and children found their dead loved ones and began to cry. Wherever their tears fell, black rocks formed—the Apache tears. Legend also has it that anyone who carries one of these stones will never need to cry again, because the Apache women have cried enough tears for all who mourn.

Cash had the Apache tear strung to wear around his neck, and he wore it throughout the recording of *Bitter Tears.* Inspired by Nancy Hayes's gift, Cash wrote the song "Apache Tears" for the album. Recounting the abuse and rape of a Native American woman at the hands of US soldiers, it's one of the most raw and gut-wrenching songs Cash ever wrote.

In addition to "As Long as the Grass Shall Grow," which opens the album, and "The Ballad of Ira Hayes," Cash covered three other Peter La Farge songs on *Bitter Tears*. The song "Custer" is an exercise in role reversal. In the song, the death of the dashing General George Armstrong Custer and the massacre of the Seventh Cavalry Unit isn't told as a courageous, if tragic, US military defeat, as Custer's Last Stand. Rather, "Custer" recounts a stunning Native American *victory* over an invading enemy. Cash sings the song with a venomous edge, cackling taunts at the slain military commander. It's no wonder *Bitter Tears* ruffled America's patriotic feathers.

La Farge's song "Drums" recounts the sad history of the Native American boarding schools, the colonial attempt to "civilize" the pagan savages. As a 2008 NPR report describes them, the reservation boarding schools were, for the US government, "a possible solution to the so-called Indian problem. [But for] the tens of thousands of Indians who went to boarding schools, it's largely remembered as a time of abuse and desecration of culture."[2] Richard Pratt, the army officer who founded the first of the Indian boarding schools, described his educational philosophy in a speech he gave in 1892: "A great general has said that the only good Indian is a dead one. . . . In a sense, I agree with the sentiment, but only in this: that all the Indian there is in the race should be dead. Kill the Indian in him, and save the man."[3] This was the education Native American children faced in the boarding schools.

The last La Farge song on the album is "White Girl," which explores the fraught and painful landscape of interracial romance and sexuality: a "white girl" flaunts and displays her Native American lover like an exotic trophy, only to discard him in the end.

Cash also contributed one other original song to the album. A spoken-word piece, "The Talking Leaves" tells the story of Sequoyah, the inventor of the Cherokee syllabary, which made reading and writing in Cherokee possible. Sequoyah had observed the white settlers communicating through marks made on paper, what Sequoyah described as "the talking leaves." In the early 1800s, wanting to give his people the ability to communicate in a way that rivaled that of the white man, Sequoyah developed eighty-six characters that match the syllables of the Cherokee language. Officially adopted by the Cherokee nation in 1825, the system rapidly spread, leading to a dramatic increase in Cherokee literacy rates—often outstripping the rates of the neighboring white settlers.

Cash closes out *Bitter Tears* with a Johnny Horton cover, "The Vanishing Race." A haunting ending to the album, it describes a Navajo brave viewing the long wagon trains encroaching upon Native American lands. Sung as a dirge, with a drum slowly beating, "The Vanishing Race" is a foreboding tune about an expanding empire and the coming genocide of indigenous peoples.

———

Bitter Tears was recorded four years before Cash's epochal live concert album at Folsom Prison, the recording most people look to when they think about Cash as a social critic. But in its combination of artistic risk taking, prophetic rage, and searing social commentary, *Bitter Tears* surpasses *At Folsom Prison*. *Bitter Tears* may be Cash's most Christian album. As Rodney Clapp writes, "*Bitter Tears* is feat of empathic imagination, a masterpiece of storytelling and stark musical artistry. It is

Cash at his most brilliant and in crucial ways his most Christian. In the biblical and Augustinian tradition, it is not denial and false innocence that gives new life. It is confession, painful as it may be, that renders personal and collective history truthfully and yet bearably, by the only means that can prevent continued or future harm."[4]

If the reception of *Bitter Tears* is any indication, Cash hit his prophetic mark a little too close to home. *Bitter Tears* got little critical attention or airplay on the radio, prompting Cash to take out the *Billboard* ad to call out a "gutless" music industry. As Cash wrote in his *Billboard* ad, "I had to fight back when I realized that so many stations are afraid of 'Ira Hayes.'" Cash also sent out hundreds of copies of "The Ballad of Ira Hayes" to DJs across the country, with a handwritten note imploring the stations to give the record a chance.

The *Billboard* ad and the mail campaign hurt a lot of feelings in the music industry. No one likes to be called "gutless." But the marketing push eventually paid off. By the end of the year, "The Ballad of Ira Hayes" got enough radio play to appear on the *Billboard* charts. Cash had burned a lot of bridges with DJs, radio owners, and music industry executives to get a hearing for the message of *Bitter Tears*. But despite the damage it did to his reputation, the fight for *Bitter Tears* became one of Cash's proudest accomplishments.

———

Bitter Tears is liberation theology according to Johnny Cash. Liberation theology grew out of the experiences of the poor and oppressed in Latin America in the 1960s and '70s, the heart of which is the claim that God has a "preferential option" for those weeping bitter tears. To be sure, liberation theology has been controversial, at times connected with Marxist and revolutionary movements. In Latin America during the sixties and seventies, there were instances where Catholic priests took up arms to fight alongside the poor. But the very best of liberation theology is seen in martyrs like Oscar Romero, who preached nonviolence but spoke out so prophetically about God's preferential concern for the poor, oppressed, and tortured in El Salvador that he was gunned down at the altar celebrating Mass.

God's preferential concern for the poor and oppressed runs through the whole of Scripture. It begins in Exodus, with God choosing to side with the slaves over the slave masters. The preferential option says God is not neutral or indifferent in these conflicts. God takes sides. Moses declares to Pharaoh, "Let my people go!" The gospel according to liberation theology is emancipation, liberation, and justice.

We also see God's preferential concern at work in the Hebrew prophets. Amos cries out, "Let justice roll on like a river, righteousness like a never-failing stream!" Isaiah indicts those who are exploiting the poor but who think, because of their fasting and religious observances, that they will find favor with God. But God blasts their hypocrisy. The prophet contrasts their pseudo-fasting with the "true fast" the Lord requires:

> Yet on the day of your fasting, you do as you please
> and exploit all your workers.
> Your fasting ends in quarreling and strife,
> and in striking each other with wicked fists.
> You cannot fast as you do today
> and expect your voice to be heard on high.

Is not this the kind of fasting I have chosen:
>to loose the chains of injustice
>and untie the cords of the yoke,
to set the oppressed free
>and break every yoke?
Is it not to share your food with the hungry
>and to provide the poor wanderer with shelter—
when you see the naked, to clothe them,
>and not to turn away from your own flesh and blood?
(Isa 58:3b–4, 6–7)

All through the Gospels, Jesus, too, proclaims the preferential option. In Luke, Jesus inaugurates his ministry by preaching his first sermon in his hometown of Nazareth. The sermon, called by some the Nazareth Manifesto, functions as a summary of Jesus's vision for the kingdom of God:

He went to Nazareth, where he had been brought up, and on the Sabbath day he went into the synagogue, as was his custom. He stood up to read, and the scroll of the prophet Isaiah was handed to him. Unrolling it, he found the place where it is written:

"The Spirit of the Lord is on me,
>because he has anointed me
>to proclaim good news to the poor.
He has sent me to proclaim freedom for the prisoners
>and recovery of sight for the blind,
>to set the oppressed free,
to proclaim the year of the Lord's favor."
(Luke 4:16–19)

"The year of the Lord's favor" referenced here is an allusion to the Year of Jubilee, the provision in the law that every fifty years, slaves are set free and economic debts forgiven (Lev 25:8–13). That is truly good news for the poor! And there is perhaps no clearer expression of God's preferential option for the poor than Jesus's blessings and woes in the Sermon on the Plain:

> Blessed are you who are poor,
>> for yours is the kingdom of God.
> . . . .
> But woe to you who are rich,
>> for you have already received your comfort.
> (Luke 6:20, 24)

Even the apostle Paul gets in on the action. For example, in 1 Corinthians 1:26–29, Paul declares:

> Brothers and sisters, think of what you were when you were called. Not many of you were wise by human standards; not many were influential; not many were of noble birth. But God chose the foolish things of the world to shame the wise; God chose the weak things of the world to shame the strong. God chose the lowly things of this world and the despised things—and the things that are not—to nullify the things that are, so that no one may boast before him.

The preferential option declares that God chooses the weak, despised, and lowly over the strong, exalted, and powerful. God takes a side. This thread runs through the entire Bible, from start to finish.

A critical practice of liberation theology is allowing the poor and oppressed to read the gospel for us. Bob Ekblad describes this as "reading the Bible with the damned."[5] When we read the gospel though God's preferential concern, we don't ask what is good news for the rich and the powerful. As Jesus said, the rich and the powerful already have their reward. Rather, the preferential option asks, What is heard as good news by the poor and oppressed?

Bitter Tears is Johnny Cash's only album that attempts to see the world, from first song to last, through the eyes of those who have been victimized. And American history looks very different when interpreted from the viewpoint of Native Americans. As *Bitter Tears* reveals, defeats become victories, heroes become oppressors, and a divinely sanctioned Manifest Destiny becomes a genocide.

So, what is the gospel? It depends upon who you ask. Pay very, very close attention to who you are asking and who you are allowing to read the Bible for you. If you ask the victors, the winners, the rich, and the powerful, you'll get one answer. If you ask the enslaved, the oppressed, the poor, and the victimized, you'll get a different one. Good news looks different, depending upon who you ask. There are rival gospels out there, and you'll have to decide which to listen to.

But the Bible's answer is clear. The gospel according to Moses, the prophets, Paul, and Jesus is this: God has a preference, God takes a side.

Moses says, "Let my people go!"

Isaiah says, "Loose the chains of injustice!"

Paul says, "God chose the weak to shame the strong!"

And Jesus says, "Blessed are the poor, and woe to the rich!"

That's a hard word; there's a reason *Bitter Tears* didn't get much airplay. But that's liberation theology according to Johnny Cash. God sides with those who are weeping bitter tears.

This is that sad song," Aidan said. My youngest son, Aidan, and I were driving to his school, listening to Johnny Cash. I had in a mix of Cash's early Sun recordings. Most casual fans only know "I Walk the Line" and "Folsom Prison Blues" from this era. And if you listen to Cash's Sun years, you don't find a lot, outside of the darkness of "Folsom Prison Blues," of what we'd consider to be a classic Johnny Cash song—those songs full of trains, Jesus, and murder. Instead, the Sun years are filled with songs of teenage romance and heartbreak. After "I Walk the Line" was released in 1956, Cash followed up with adolescent weepers like "There You Go" and "Home of the Blues," along with bubblegum pop songs like "Ballad of a Teenage Queen."

This music is a far cry from the murderous lament of "Folsom Prison Blues," but it's the music that Sam Phillips wanted. In 1956, Elvis, who had jumped from Sun to RCA, was in the midst of his meteoric rise, dominating the record charts and silver screen with songs like "Heartbreak Hotel," "Hound Dog," and "Love Me

Tender." At Sun, Jerry Lee Lewis was soon to score big with his song "Whole Lotta Shakin' Goin' On." From Sun's perspective, it only made sense to move Cash toward the teenage pop sound that was so hot.

But that sound wasn't Johnny Cash. Significantly, for the first time, as he suffered through a songwriting lull searching for his next "I Walk the Line," Cash wasn't writing many of the songs he was recording. Cash felt increasingly alienated from his music. He wasn't being true to himself. The songs lacked grit, authenticity, and emotional depth. He didn't care about these songs.

And then he had a breakthrough. He wrote a very sad song.

———

The origin of that song, "Give My Love to Rose," occurred on one of Cash's tours. After a show in California, a man approached Cash backstage. The man was an ex-convict, just released from prison, eager to get back to his home in Shreveport to see his wife. But he was broke and jobless, with dim prospects for getting work due to his criminal history. Knowing that Cash played the Louisiana Hayride in Shreveport, he asked if Cash would give his love to his wife, should see her first.

The tragedy of the request haunted Cash, and he used that memory to write "Give My Love to Rose." In the song, the narrator finds a man dying by the railroad tracks. The narrator goes to the man and kneels over him in his final moments. The man shares that he's an ex-convict trying to make it back home to his wife and son, and he shares his final, dying request:

Give my love to Rose please won't you, Mister
Take her all my money, tell her to buy some pretty clothes
Tell my boy that daddy's so proud of him
And don't forget to give my love to Rose.

I agree with Aidan, "Give My Love to Rose" is a very sad song. And it became a pivotal song in Cash's career. He knew that a song about an ex-convict dying on the railroad tracks wasn't going to be a huge seller like "I Walk the Line," but it was a song that Cash deeply cared about. It began a tradition with Cash. From this point on, he began to discriminate between "Johnny Cash songs" and "J.R. Cash songs." A Johnny Cash song was one like "Ballad of a Teenage Queen," a fun, superficial song meant to sell records. But a J.R. Cash song, by contrast, was a song that meant something to Cash, a song that took him back to his roots. J.R. songs might not sell very well (songs about dying, homeless convicts rarely do), but they gave voice to Cash's artistic and spiritual vision.

"Give My Love to Rose" made the artist we call the Man in Black. "Folsom Prison Blues" had laid the first stone; its sociopathic and depressing tone in the midst of the teenage pop dominating the airwaves was a sign that something was different about Cash. Johnny Cash could take you to some very dark places, in a way that Elvis and Jerry Lee Lewis never dared. But the artistic promise of "Folsom Prison Blues" needed to be followed up, and with Sun pushing Cash for more teenage weepers, Cash could have gotten lost. Artistically, he could have kept chasing the next big hit, increasingly singing songs written by others. Instead, Cash wrote a sad song about a convict who dies on the railroad tracks, never making it back home to his family.

As expected, "Give My Love to Rose" didn't sell very well, but it fulfilled the early promise of "Folsom Prison Blues." With "Give My Love to Rose," Cash had figured out who he was as an artist. True, he never stopped aspiring to write hits like "I Walk the Line," but Cash recognized the contrast between the music that sold and paid the bills and the music that was most meaningful to him—the music that gave voice to the outcasts, the downtrodden, and the broken.

The origin of the song "Give My Love to Rose"—Cash's approachability and willingness to help an ex-convict pass on his love to his wife—illustrates another aspect of Cash's ability to show solidarity in his life and his music. As Marshall Grant described it, the thing Johnny Cash was most addicted to in his life was "trying to do good."[1] On tours, Cash would buy extra groceries and give them away if he saw someone on the down and out. When Cash found out about fans who had driven long distances to attend one of his concerts, he would often pay for their meals and hotel rooms. Cash regularly gave money away. As Grant observed, "He'd give you the shirt off his back, and if he was straight, everything else he had in his possession."[2]

John Carter Cash vividly recounts a story from his childhood that highlights Cash's kindness and compassion. Johnny, June, and John Carter were driving in a car in New York City when a large rock was thrown through the window, sending shards of shattered glass over June. Johnny Cash grabbed the rock and stormed out of the car to confront the person who had thrown it. He rushed up to the perpetrator, a shirtless young man who had a dazed, blank look in his eyes. "Is this your rock?" Cash furiously demanded, holding out the rock.

The man addressed Cash incoherently, with a heavy accent and garbled English. Cash stared, facing the man eye to eye, and for a moment John Carter Cash felt his father was going to hit the man. Instead, John Carter Cash recounts what happened next:

> Then Dad held out the rock again. "Take it," he said. . . .
>
> "Go put this back where you found it, please," said my father, and then turned his back and walked back to the car.
>
> "Good Lord, John . . . What on earth was wrong with that young man?"
>
> "I think he was on drugs, June," answered my dad. "I don't even think he knew where he was . . . Let's pray for him."
>
> And so my mother and father got out of the car and walked over to the man . . . I saw my father bend down on one knee, and then my mother with him. As they prayed, the man closed his eyes and began to cry.[3]

Reflecting on his father and that incident, John Carter Cash shares, "My father was a gentle man."

———

When we talk about solidarity, we tend to think of structural oppressions and of political and economic injustices. Being in solidarity gets reduced to being a social-justice warrior. To be sure, God's preferential option for the poor demands we fight against systemic evil.

And as we've noted, Cash prophetically spoke out about systemic injustices in *At Folsom Prison* (the plight of the incarcerated) and *Bitter Tears* (the plight of the Native Americans). But the drama of solidarity that plays out in "Give My Love to Rose" is more intimate, more personal. Solidarity isn't just expressed in prophetic speech and action but also in acts of tenderness, gentleness, and kindness—like passing on the final request of a man dying alone on the railroad tracks or praying for the addict who just threw a rock through your car window. The gospel according to Johnny Cash calls us to kindness.

Yet the kindness of "Give My Love to Rose" doesn't come easily to us. I don't know if I could have done what Cash did that day in New York. Kindness—at least the sort of kindness that Jesus calls us to—is difficult.

I was once at a conference with pastor and author Brian Zahnd, who was sharing about his book *Beauty Will Save the World*. The title of Brian's book comes from a quote from the Russian novelist Dostoyevsky. Brian's point was that people, even many atheists, find Jesus beautiful. People might not like organized religion or Christianity, but they find Jesus beautiful. So, Brian argued, we must present Jesus to the world. His beauty will save it.

I make a similar argument in my book *Stranger God*, connecting the beauty of Jesus to his kindness. "Random acts of kindness" always seem to go viral on social media. In *Stranger God*, I recount two of these social-media stories. One is about an old woman who reached out to take the hand of a crazy, threatening man on a Canadian subway, her tender act soothing and calming him. The other is a story of a star Florida State football player who, while visiting a school, broke away from the team to share lunch with an autistic boy eating alone. Both of these stories of kindness went viral, as have thousands of others on social media. As I share in *Stranger God*, these stories go viral because they point us toward Jesus:

> Our hearts thrill to the stories of kindness on social media because they remind us of Jesus. We see that seventy-year-old woman take the hand of a screaming crazy man, and we think of Jesus' kindness to those possessed by devils. We see the football player eating lunch with an autistic boy, and we think of Jesus touching lepers. We read these stories of kindness on social media, and our hearts leap in a flash of recognition: *That is exactly the sort of thing Jesus would have done.*[4]

I agree with Brian; this is the beauty that will save the world. But the more I've reflected on it, the more I've wondered if we are attracted to Jesus as much as we think. For example, Jesus's contemporaries didn't seem to find his kindness all that beautiful. In fact, they found his kindness to sinners, tax collectors, and prostitutes offensive. And I can't help but think that's the same sort of reaction I would have had if I were living in Jesus's day.

Yes, Jesus's beauty will save the world, but there is something transgressive about this beauty. *Transgressive* is a word from the art community, used to describe artwork that goes against our artistic, aesthetic sensibilities. Transgressive art shocks, offends, and startles us. In a similar way, Jesus displays a transgressive beauty, a beauty that moves through the world in a way that shocks, offends, and startles us—mainly because Jesus's kindness stands in solidarity with people we'd rather ignore and exclude. Jesus practices a transgressive kindness.

I was reminded of the transgressive nature of Jesus's kindness when I read George Saunders's convocation speech delivered at Syracuse University for the class of 2013. The theme of Saunders's speech was what he regretted most about his life. After surveying his poor jobs, bad decisions, and embarrassing moments, each a possible contender for "greatest regret in life," Saunders shared a story from his childhood. When Saunders was in the seventh grade, a new girl came to his school. "Ellen" (Saunders doesn't use her real name) was small, shy, wore uncool glasses, and had a habit of chewing a strand of her hair when she was nervous. Ellen didn't fit in, and she became an object of ridicule and teasing. Saunders remembers Ellen standing in her front yard, scared, lonely, and friendless in the neighborhood. He continues:

> And then—they moved. That was it. No tragedy, no big final hazing.
>
> One day she was there, next day she wasn't.
>
> End of story.
>
> Now, why do I regret *that*? Why, forty-two years later, am I still thinking about it? Relative to most of the other kids, I was actually pretty *nice* to her. . . .
>
> But still. It bothers me.
>
> So here's something I know to be true, although it's a little corny, and I don't quite know what to do with it: what I regret most in my life are *failures of kindness*.[5]

We all have Ellens in our life. And these failures of kindness are caused by the transgressive nature of kindness, how kindness calls us to go against the social grain. We find kindness beautiful when we see it in others, but far too often, we don't practice it ourselves. We thrill to these stories on social media, but most of the people on that Canadian subway that day stepped away from the crazy man. Only one woman took his hand. And most of the Florida State football players sat with the team that day in the cafeteria. Only one player broke away to eat with an autistic boy sitting alone.

The kindness we're called to practice isn't easy or natural. It's actually pretty heroic and rare—which is why it's so viral. As an act of solidarity with the Ellens of the world, kindness involves moving toward others when most, ourselves included, would rather back away.

———

Still, the tender, intimate kindness of "Give My Love to Rose," while sentimental and sweet, can seem small and insignificant to those of us who are raging and waging a battle against the forces of systemic oppression in the world. Whenever I preach about kindness, the social-justice warriors in the room grow impatient. Are these small acts of compassion really enough to change a world that seems increasingly out of control? "Give My Love to Rose" doesn't seem to be the anthem the revolution is looking for.

Yet any revolution devoid of tenderness is destined to become depersonalized and dehumanized in various ways. It's far easier to love issues than actual human beings. I know lots of social-justice warrior types who rage against oppression on social media but are missing in action in their neighborhoods when it comes to loving people in personal, concrete, and intimate ways. For example, I have lots of progressive friends who care a lot—on social media at least—about poverty and income inequality, but who have never welcomed a homeless person into their home for a meal. There is more to following Jesus than voting well every four years.

Devoid of kindness, political movements will dehumanize our opponents as well. Our rage needs to be seasoned with love, and the best way to do that is through kindness. As Paul encourages in Romans 12:20, "If your enemy is hungry, feed him; if he is thirsty, give him something to drink. In doing this, you will heap burning coals on his head."

Finally, lasting social change is often won or lost in the intimate spaces of a community trying to live in solidarity with others, in the small acts of sharing and serving. Kindness cultivates a joyful, attractive, and sustainable community of resistance. As the saying goes, "Everyone wants a revolution, but nobody wants to do the dishes." The kindness of doing the dishes sustains the long faithfulness required to bring God's kingdom to earth as it is in heaven. All that to say, I've come to think that kindness is the revolution we've all been looking for, the heart and soul of God's strategy to save the world.

The Old Testament book of Ruth preaches us that message. The book is a sweet, intimate story of two acts of kindness. It opens with Naomi, an Israelite who has moved to Moab with her husband and two sons to avoid a famine. While they are in Moab, Naomi's two sons marry Moabite women. Tragically, all of the husbands die, leaving Naomi and her two daughters-in-law in a precarious situation—especially Naomi, living in a foreign land. Naomi tells her daughters-in-law, one of whom is Ruth, to go back to their own people as she returns back to Israel.

The first act of kindness in the story is Ruth's pledge to stay with Naomi, to accompany her back to Israel, and never to leave her. Ruth makes her pledge with some of the most famous, poetic, and moving words in all of the Bible:

"Don't urge me to leave you
    or to turn back from you.
Where you go I will go,
    and where you stay I will stay.
Your people will be my people
    and your God my God.
Where you die I will die,
    and there I will be buried.
May the Lord deal with me,
    be it ever so severely,
if even death separates you and me."
(Ruth 1:16–17)

So Ruth and Naomi return to Israel.

The second act of kindness in the story happens when Naomi sends Ruth out to glean in the fields of Boaz, a family relation. It's harvest season, so Boaz is busy and harried trying to manage it all. But in the midst of that chaos, he does something surprising. He notices a lone woman, gleaning all by herself, behind all his workers. The woman is obviously poor, unattached, and very vulnerable.

I find Boaz's noticing Ruth remarkable. Ruth is the *last* person Boaz should have noticed in the midst of a busy harvest. He's got plenty of his own people and workers, who need and demand his attention. But Boaz sees Ruth. The person everyone is ignoring, he notices.

To go back to George Saunders's story, this is Boaz's Ellen moment. It's a "Give My Love to Rose" moment. It's the moment to extend a transgressive, unlikely kindness. And Boaz passes the test. Approaching this very vulnerable woman, Boaz covers Ruth with kindness: "My daughter, listen to me. Don't go and glean in another field and don't go away from here. Stay here with the women who work for me. Watch the field where the men are harvesting, and follow along after the women. I have told the men not to lay a hand on you. And whenever you are thirsty, go and get a drink from the water jars the men have filled" (Ruth 2:8–9).

The book of Ruth is a tender story of two kindnesses. It's a small and intimate story of little people doing little things. And what I find so powerful about the story is how it begins: "In the days when the judges ruled." That's a significant opening. Have you read the book of Judges recently? I wouldn't recommend it. That book is *awful*. It is the story of Israel's slow, tragic decline into political chaos and moral depravity. Judges ends with what is perhaps the most horrific story in the entire Bible. (I'll spare you the gory details, but you can read the story in Judges 19.)

The setting of Ruth during the time of the judges is profound and convicting. During the time of the judges, the world was falling apart. There was moral and political corruption. Evil and chaos reigned. And isn't that *exactly* how a lot of us feel about our world right now? The center isn't holding. All is falling into darkness. Political oppression is everywhere. Moral decay is all around us.

Yet in the middle of all that chaos and confusion, the Bible zooms in to tell a tender, intimate story of kindness. During the time when the judges ruled, Ruth made a promise to Naomi—a small thing when the world is falling apart. And during the time when the judges ruled, Boaz saw Ruth on the edge of his field—a small thing, to cover her with kindness, when the world is spinning out of control. And so it seems to us today. Can our small acts of kindness really make a difference, given all the chaos and corruption going on around us?

The reason why the Bible zooms in on the small acts of kindness in the book of Ruth comes at the end of the story. Ruth and Boaz eventually get married, and they have a son named Obed. And Obed goes on to have a son named Jesse. And Jesse, you might recall, has a very famous son: King David. Because of two acts of kindness, Boaz and Ruth become the great-grandparents of King David. And we know of another famous child who came into the world because of this kindness. Boaz and Ruth are the great, great, great . . . great-grandparents of Jesus.

The moral of the story? It's this: during the time when the judges ruled, God used kindness to save the world.

Yes, the world is out of control. This is a time when the judges are ruling. The problems we are facing are large, complex, systemic, and intractable. And here we are, little people with little lives, making little choices. Can our small acts of kindness make any difference?

Does it make any difference to become friends with Ellen? To reach out and take the hand of a crazy man on a subway? To eat lunch with an autistic child? To carry the last wish of a man dying alone on the railroad tracks? To pray for the man who threw a rock through your car window?

Can kindness really make a difference? Boaz, Ruth, and the Man in Black know the answer. This is the beauty that will save the world.

CHAPTER 9

"THE LEGEND OF JOHN HENRY'S HAMMER"

Cotton grows inside a hard, golf-ball-size shell called a cotton boll. Early in the fall, the boll opens up and dries, exposing the cotton fibers within. The opened boll becomes a cotton burr, which has four or five sharp spurs on it. The cotton sits in the middle of these spurs, which are the bane of the cotton picker. If you're not careful, the cotton burr pricks and cuts the fingertips as you reach for the cotton to pull it out of the burr. Experienced cotton pickers carry scars on their fingers from their years of working in the cotton fields.

Johnny Cash's fingers carried the scars of the cotton burrs. Whenever he looked down at his hands as he was playing his guitar, he was reminded of his humble roots working on the family farm in Dyess, Arkansas. Cash summed up his childhood in Dyess this way: "Jesus Was Our Savior—Cotton Was Our King."[1]

Cash sang about cotton farming all his life, often describing it to his urban audiences. During his live concert album recorded at Madison Square Garden in 1969, Cash explains to the city slickers how "fair to middling" is a grade of cotton. A cotton crop is graded on the strength, length, color, smoothness, and uniformity of the fibers. "Fair to middling" is an average grade. Cotton farming is the source of the Southern idiom that when you're doing fine, you're doing "fair to middlin'."

On the Dyess farm, the Cash family planted their cotton in April. After planting, they weeded and prayed, petitioning the Lord for six whole months that the Mississippi River wouldn't flood them out, that army worms wouldn't infest and kill the crop, or that some other natural disaster wouldn't be visited upon them. Cotton farming was a precarious life.

If their prayers were answered, in October the blossoms would appear on the four-foot-high plants. Picking began soon after that, made easier if there had been a hard frost, stripping the leaves off the plants and making the burrs easier to see. The family picked into December, until the winter rains came and ruined the quality of the cotton.

After the hard initial work of clearing the land for farming, the first few years on the Dyess farm were good years for the cotton. During those years, the fields yielded the Cash family two bales to the acre of highly graded "strict high middling" cotton. By the time Cash got to high school, however, the good cotton crops were a thing of the past. With the family unable to afford fertilizer, the soil on the Cash farm gradually became depleted. Cotton farming struggled, and many Dyess farmers gave up. Ray Cash, however, kept at it, rotating his crops to keep the soil from degrading. Still, the best years of the farm were behind them. Farming got harder and harder.

Little J.R. started in the cotton fields as a water boy, lugging water to the older family members picking in the fields. By the time he was eight, he picked, dragging behind him the heavy six- or nine-foot-long canvas sack in which they stuffed the cotton. Cotton picking is backbreaking work—hours and hours spent bending over the short cotton plants. Putting in a hard ten hours in the field, J.R. could pick two hundred to three hundred pounds of cotton.

J.R. hated those burrs, how they cut and pricked his hands. After the first days picking in the fields, J.R.'s hands were red, covered with tiny cuts and wounds. At least it was a shared experience: everyone in the family and the Dyess community carried the cuts of the cotton burrs. Cash remembered his sisters crying in the fields from the pain.

Johnny Cash was born at the start of the Great Depression, and the poverty of those years profoundly shaped his music. When we speak about themes of solidarity in the music and art of Johnny Cash, we have to mention the Man in Black's ability to speak for and to the poor and working classes. These were Cash's people. Cash knew poverty. He had the scars on his fingers to prove it.

Cash sang his entire life about the dignity of the poor and working classes. Johnny Cash's music was a love song to the economically downtrodden and disenfranchised. Examples of this from Cash's oeuvre abound, but the best example is Cash's second concept album, *Blood, Sweat and Tears*, released in 1963.

When Cash joined Columbia Records, after leaving Sam Phillips and Sun, he was given greater creative freedom. In addition to recording gospel albums, Cash exercised greater control over his artistic vision and released a suite of concept albums in the early sixties. These albums don't contain many of what we'd describe as Cash's "greatest hits," but they are, as a group, the heart and soul of Johnny Cash's music.

If you really want to get to know the music of J.R. Cash, the boy who grew up picking cotton in Dyess, Arkansas, don't listen to a greatest-hits compilation. Listen to these four albums: *Ride This Train*, a narrated train ride through America filled with story and song, was the first concept album, released in 1960. *Blood, Sweat and Tears*, Cash's ode to the working classes, followed in 1963. *Bitter Tears*, the protest album concerning the plight of Native Americans, appeared in 1964. And *Sings the Ballads of the True West*, Cash's love song to the cowboys, drifters, outlaws, and gamblers of Old West, came out in 1965. Cash would go on to record other concept albums, but these four albums, appearing in such quick succession in the early sixties, represent the creative peak of Cash's musical career.

Clocking in at just over thirty minutes, the nine tracks of *Blood, Sweat and Tears* highlight the dignity and suffering of the working classes in America. The songs "Tell Him I'm Gone," "Another Man Done Gone," and "Chain Gang" tell the story of "convict lease," a form of state-sponsored slavery in America in which prisoners were used as a labor source for private companies. The practice flourished in the South after the Civil War, as industries sought cheap labor after the end of slavery. The work conditions for convict lease prisoners were abysmal and frequently deadly.

The story of Martin Tabert illustrates the horrors. In 1921, Tabert, a twenty-two-year-old man from North Dakota, was arrested in Tallahassee, Florida, for riding on a train without a ticket. Convicted of vagrancy and ordered to pay a fine of twenty-five dollars or spend three months in jail, he contacted his parents, who wired the money to the county office. But due to a mix-up with the wiring, the money never came through. Having failed to pay the fine, Tabert was soon transferred, per a convict lease agreement, to a work camp in Dixie County, sixty miles south of Tallahassee. At the camp, he was assigned to the Putnam Lumber Company to clear timber in the Florida swamps.

In the swamps, Tabert contracted malaria, resulting in fevers, headaches, and oozing sores. Unable to complete a day's work, Tabert had to face the work camp punishment. Walter Higginbotham, the whipping boss, propped up the prisoner on his swollen feet and flogged him fifty times with a heavy leather strap. Tabert tried to plead for mercy but was so weak he could barely talk. Higginbotham beat Tabert into unconsciousness. The company doctor was summoned to examine the unconscious Tabert. The doctor diagnosed the malaria, but it didn't matter. Tabert died later that night.

"Busted" is one of the standout songs on *Blood, Sweat and Tears*. Cash used the song for his live concert at Folsom Prison. While the tune of "Busted" is energetic and upbeat, the lyrics of the song are full of desperation in the face of poverty—failed crops, sick children, a stack of bills. The father in the song has to face the shame of begging and is tempted to steal to take care of his family.

Other songs on *Blood, Sweat and Tears* tell the stories of various blue-collar jobs and heroes, including coal miner ("Nine Pound Hammer"), train conductor ("Casey Jones"), and oil field worker ("Roughneck").

The song Cash was most proud of on *Blood, Sweat and Tears* was "The Legend of John Henry's Hammer," about the famous African

American folk hero who beat a steam engine in a race to tunnel through a mountain. The song remains as relevant today as it was then, featuring an incarcerated father, unpaid medical bills, crushing generational poverty, racism, and the creeping displacement of human labor by machines. As John Henry laments:

"I feed four little brothers.
And baby sister's walkin' on her knees.
Did the Lord say that machines ought to take place of livin'?
And what's a substitute for bread and beans? I ain't seen it!
Do engines get rewarded for their steam?"

"John Henry" clocked in at over eight minutes, making it unlikely that the song would get much radio play. It was a J.R. song, recorded not for commercial success but for the meaning it held for Cash. Cash made "The Legend of John Henry's Hammer" the centerpiece of *Blood, Sweat and Tears,* his anthem to the American workingman.

———

Blood, Sweat and Tears and *Ride This Train* are the clearest expressions of the Man in Black's solidarity with the poor and economically disadvantaged. In *Blood, Sweat and Tears* and *Ride This Train,* we are back in Dyess, Arkansas. We are living in the middle of the Great Depression. We are facing, as in the song "Busted," the emotional despair and the morally corrosive effects of poverty. This is the music that makes your fingers bleed from the cotton burrs. As Quentin Tarantino observes in the liner notes of *God, Love, Murder,* "In a country that thinks it's divided by race, where actually it's divided by economics, Johnny Cash's songs of hillbilly thug life go right to the heart of the American underclass."[2]

The call to economic solidarity in *Blood, Sweat and Tears* continues to be a pressing concern. Nationally and internationally, income and wealth inequity continue to increase, with corrosive effects upon our souls, bodies, minds, families, communities, and nation. The social contract binding our nation together will disintegrate if the distance between the haves and have-nots continues to widen.

Jesus talked about money more than anything else; he called it God's one true rival in the world. "No one can serve two masters," Jesus says in Matthew 6:24. "Either you will hate the one and love the other, or you will be devoted to the one and despise the other. You cannot serve both God and money." Jesus also flatly declared, "It is hard for someone who is rich to enter the kingdom of heaven" (Matthew 19:23). The apostle Paul underlines the sentiment: "For the love of money is a root of all kinds of evil. Some people, eager for money, have wandered from the faith and pierced themselves with many griefs" (1 Tim 6:10).

Pope Francis, in his apostolic exhortation *Evangelii Gaudium* (The Joy of the Gospel), describes how our world is being governed by "economies of exclusion," with increasingly harmful effects upon those at the bottom. Francis writes:

> Just as the commandment "Thou shalt not kill" sets a clear limit in order to safeguard the value of human life, today we also have to say "thou shalt not" to an economy of exclusion and inequality. Such an economy kills. How can it be that it is not a news item when an elderly homeless person dies

of exposure, but it is news when the stock market loses two points? . . . Today everything comes under the laws of competition and the survival of the fittest, where the powerful feed upon the powerless. As a consequence, masses of people find themselves excluded and marginalized: without work, without possibilities, without any means of escape.

Human beings are themselves considered consumer goods to be used and then discarded.[3]

These are the lethal economic conditions that Cash witnessed firsthand in Dyess and that he sings about in *Blood, Sweat and Tears*. Little has changed.

John Henry, the hero in Cash's ode to the workingman, is African American. We tend to treat race and class as separate issues in American politics, but the two are deeply intertwined. Our persistent lack of progress in healing our racial divisions in America is rooted in the unjust economic legacies that have been bequeathed to us. Martin Luther King Jr., after historic victories in securing civil and voting rights in 1964 and '65, turned his attention to poverty and economic justice for just this reason. In a move that is little remembered today, King left the South to live in a Chicago slum. In the North, King faced huge resistance from city officials and local residents when he marched and fought for equal-housing measures. Economic solidarity is costly for those benefiting from the status quo, so it is the most difficult solidarity to express. King observed in Chicago that he was a moral hero when he marched against white racists in the South but widely vilified in the North when he turned his attention to economics. The moral hypocrisy of white liberals in the North shocked and depressed King. His call for equal housing hit, quite literally, a little too close to home.

In all this, the music of *Blood, Sweat and Tears* remains profoundly relevant. The economies of exclusion that the white farmers faced in Dyess and Martin Luther King Jr. faced in the Chicago slums are still very much with us. The poor continue to swim in rivers of blood, sweat, and tears.

—

Beyond a call for economic solidarity, Cash's music also gave dignity, honor, and human recognition to the poor. In the meritocracy that is the American dream, being poor is shameful. Poverty is taken to be symptomatic of inferiority. The poor are looked down on as psychologically or morally broken. The poor are lazy, unintelligent, dishonest, or lacking in self-control. They are addicts and welfare cheats. Why else, in this land of opportunity, would they be poor? Deeply embedded in the American psyche rests the belief that if you are honest and hardworking, you simply cannot be poor. It's an impossibility. The American dream *always* rewards the good and punishes the wicked.

Johnny Cash knew this was a lie. While Cash had issues with his father after Jack's death, he knew his father was honest and a hard worker, as were most of the farmers in the Dyess community. But that honesty and hard work—all the blood, sweat, and tears—did little to keep the creditors from calling. The poor families of Dyess carried a shame and stigma they didn't deserve. Yes, they were poor, but they were good, honest, decent folk.

Knowing this and bearing the scars on his own fingers to prove it, Johnny Cash spent his entire career exposing the lie. He devoted his music to singing honor and dignity back into the poor. In many ways, Cash's entire career was a love song to Dyess.

—

In 1 Corinthians, the apostle Paul calls upon the church to sing honor and dignity back into the poor. Recall that the church of Corinth was filled with the poor and uneducated: "Not many of you were wise by human standards; not many were influential; not many were of noble birth" (1 Cor 1:26). Unfortunately, many of the wealthier members of the Corinthian church were shaming their poorer brothers and sisters. Paul attacks this shaming, commanding that the church show "special honor" to those suffering economic and social marginalization within Roman society. Here are his words from 1 Corinthians, supplemented with some commentary from me in italics:

> The eye cannot say to the hand, "I don't need you!" And the head cannot say to the feet, "I don't need you!" *[This was how the rich were treating the poor members of the church, as unwanted and disposable.]* On the contrary, those parts of the body that seem to be weaker *[the poor members]* are indispensable, and the parts that we think are less honorable *[the people shamed by Roman society]* we treat with special honor. And the parts that are unpresentable *[the poor, shameful members]* are treated with special modesty, while our presentable parts *[the wealthy and influential members of*

the church] need no special treatment. But God has put the body together, giving greater honor to the parts that lacked it *[the poor and shameful]*, so that there should be no division in the body, but that its parts *[the rich and the poor]* should have equal concern for each other. If one part suffers, every part suffers with it; if one part is honored, every part rejoices with it. (1 Cor 12: 21–26)

That's the gospel according to Johnny Cash, singing honor and dignity back into the poor and disadvantaged. Solidarity with the poor calls for economic justice, but it also shows up in the small, personal, and intimate ways we extend honor and shame. In the words of Paul, the church gives greater honor to those who lack it.

Through his music, Johnny Cash gave special honor to those who lacked it. Honor for the Native Americans in *Bitter Tears*. Honor for the prisoners in *At Folsom Prison*. And honor for those who have scarred fingers from years of picking cotton. That's the gospel according to Johnny Cash: special honor for those who live and die in blood, sweat, and tears.

CHAPTER 10

"SUNDAY MORNIN' COMING DOWN"

The devil came to Johnny Cash in 1957 in the form of a little white pill marked, ironically, with a cross. The pill was an amphetamine, a Benzedrine tablet. And so began a life-or-death struggle that haunted Johnny Cash for the rest of his life.

The reference to the devil is not an exaggeration. Cash always spoke of his addiction as a form of demon possession. In a 1970 interview, Cash described his life on drugs:

> It was like I was living with a bunch of demons. I don't want to get deep into demons 'cause I don't know that much about demonology, but I used to get into the desert and start talking to them. I'd talk to the demons and they'd talk back to me—and I could hear them. I mean, they'd say, "Go on, John, take twenty more milligrams of Dexedrine, you'll be all right." And I'd say, "Yeah, but I've already had forty today." And they'd answer, "Take twenty more, it'll be good for you, it'll make you feel just fine." So I'd take 'em

and then continue talking back and forth to the demons inside me.[1]

During the mid-1970s, after almost twenty years of heavy drug use, Cash had stabilized and sobered up. The demons were quiet, and Cash's life seemed back on track. He had re-devoted himself to his family and to God, and he was recording and filming *The Gospel Road*, a feature film about the life of Jesus. He started writing *Man in White*, a biography about the life of the apostle Paul. In his 1975 autobiography, *Man in Black*, Cash presents this period of his life as a classic tent-revival testimony, a story of redemption and salvation. He had descended into sin, madness, and hopelessness, and he had been rescued and restored by God.

Yet Cash's sobriety in the seventies was short-lived. Cash fell off the wagon many times after that season of sobriety. In 1983, Cash's family had to stage an intervention to get him checked into the Betty Ford Center. Within six months of being released from Betty Ford, Cash had started taking pills again. In 1989, Cash entered rehab again. As any addict will tell you, the demons are not so easily exorcised. Bono, lead singer of U2, recalled visiting Cash in the late eighties at his home in Hendersonville, Tennessee. Saying grace for the meal, Cash offered up a beautifully worded, heartfelt, spiritual prayer. After the prayer was over, Cash looked up with a devilish look in his eye and said, "Sure miss the drugs, though."[2]

———

Amphetamines were common during the early years of rock 'n' roll. Without tour buses or road crews, the performers drove themselves from concert to concert, often through the night to get to the next show. The uppers helped them stay awake, and pills popped before the concerts gave sleep-deprived performers the boost they needed to put on a good show.

While Cash had picked up smoking and drinking during his years in the military, the little white pill he took in 1957 was a revelation. Amazed at how much the pills helped him put on a great show, Cash was soon taking five to ten pills a day. To keep his supply stocked on tour, he developed a routine. Upon arriving in a new town, he'd pull out the phone book and ring up a local doctor. He'd say something like, "Doc, this is Johnny Cash. I'm on a long tour and need to do some night driving. I need some of those diet pills to keep me awake." Happy to help, the doctor would write up a prescription, and Cash would get his pills. Soon he was up to twenty pills a day.

Along with alcohol and marijuana, Cash started to regulate his energy and moods by counteracting his amphetamine use with barbiturates. He popped uppers when he needed to be awake or energized and downers when he needed to calm himself or sleep. His life metamorphosed into a chemistry experiment as he manipulated his mood, energy, and sleep by taking pills as the need or occasion demanded. Slowly, he became physically, emotionally, and spiritually unmoored. The demons had found a home.

As his addiction deepened, those close to Cash noted increasingly erratic and dangerous behaviors. His once kind and generous personality changed in harsh and alarming ways. Once, he got into a fistfight with his younger brother Tommy in front of their parents. "I saw his personality change," Tommy shared about those years, "He became filled with paranoia and anger."[3] Cash trashed hotel rooms, wrecked car after car, and under the influence started a fire that destroyed 508 acres of the Los Padres National Forest.

Cash was married to Vivian during these years, and his addiction played a large part in her decision to file for divorce in 1967. Cash's four daughters—Rosanne, Kathy, Cindy, and Tara—also noticed the change in their father. Once warm and available, he grew aloof and distant, locking himself in his office and snapping at them. Rosanne summed it up best: "It just got to where it was like somebody else was coming home, not my daddy."[4]

The drug use affected his music as well. Many concerts were canceled, and promoters didn't want to schedule him. Heavy amphetamine use also causes dehydration, leading to laryngitis. The iconic voice from the early Sun years, the one that sounded like a freight train rolling down the tracks to the *boom-chicka-boom* rhythm, grew raspy and weak. Recording sessions had to be canceled, and the vocals on his albums deteriorated. Just compare any album from the sixties with Cash's vocals from the Sun years on songs like "I Walk the Line" and "Folsom Prison Blues." The change in his vocals is startling. At Carnegie Hall in 1962, a concert Cash expected to be the crowning achievement of his career up to that point, he was humiliated on the stage when he completely lost his voice. He also lost an alarming amount of weight during this time. On the cover of *Bitter Tears*, Cash looks like a skeleton, emaciated from the heavy drug use. Years later, seeing a picture of himself from this period of his life, Cash said to his son John Carter, "That is a very sick man."[5]

A low point came in 1965, when Cash was arrested in El Paso. Unable to supply his habit from doctors' prescriptions alone, Cash was buying drugs in Mexico, crossing over into Juarez when he traveled through El Paso. On October 5, Cash was arrested in El Paso with hundreds of Dexedrine and Equanil pills in his possession. A picture of a handcuffed Cash being escorted from the courthouse by US Marshals splashed across American newspapers.

During his darkest days, Cash's friends and band resigned themselves to the belief that he was eventually going to kill himself. They often found Cash unconscious and unresponsive. Every morning on tour, they expected to find him dead. Once Luther Perkins had to administer mouth-to-mouth resuscitation to get an unconscious Cash breathing again. Cash kept bouncing back enough to put on a show here and there, between the many cancellations, but it seemed only a matter of time before his luck would run out. One night, he was going to take one handful of pills too many. And that would be the end.

—

Beyond describing his addiction as a form of demon possession, Johnny Cash also described it as form of idolatry, as a failure to put God first in his life. Biblically, there is a connection between the two, demons and idolatry. An interesting example of this connection is observed in one of the biblical names for the devil. In the Gospels, Satan is called Beelzebub, meaning the Prince of Demons. We're not sure where that name comes from, but some scholars think it comes from a Canaanite god named in a story from 2 Kings. In the story, Ahaziah, king of Israel, suffers a fall and gets hurt. Seeking healing, Ahaziah doesn't turn to the God of Israel, but instead, "he sent messengers, saying to them, 'Go and consult Baal-Zebub, the god of Ekron, to see if I will recover from this injury'" (2 Kings 1:2). Instead of turning to Yahweh, the God of Israel, Ahaziah turns to the Canaanite god Baal-Zebub. Baal is the word for Lord, and Zebub is the word for flies. Baal-Zebub literally means the Lord of the Flies. And that's who the king of Israel turned to for relief.

Baal-Zebub becoming Beelzebub—the Lord of the Flies becoming the Prince of Demons—illustrates the close association between idolatry and the demonic in the Bible. When we are hurt or suffering, where do we turn? What are we leaning on to make it through the day? Where are we placing our trust? We face a choice here: God or Beelzebub? Will we turn to Jesus or the Lord of the Flies? As Johnny Cash can testify, whenever and wherever in our lives we don't put God first, there will be a buzzing sound, a swarm of flies in our hearts where we've been turning away from God and toward Beelzebub.

This talk about a choice between God and the devil may seem heavy-handed. But Cash sang about the devil his whole career, and he viewed his lifelong battle with addiction, among his other struggles, in these very terms. During the 1968–1971 run of his musical variety show on ABC, Cash felt compelled to share with his viewing audience the stark choice we all face in life: Will it be God or the devil? Against the advice of the show producers and TV executives, Cash read the following statement on national television:

> All my life I have believed that there are two powerful forces, the force of good and the force of evil, the force of right and the force of wrong, or, if you will, the force of God and the force of the devil. Well now, the force of God is naturally the Number One most powerful force, although the Number

Two most powerful force, the devil, takes over every once in a while. And he can make it pretty rough on you when he tries to take over. I know.

In my time, I fought him, I fought back, I clawed, I kicked him. When I didn't have the strength, I gnawed him. Well, here lately I think we've made the devil pretty mad because on our show we've been mentioning God's name. . . . Well, this probably made the devil pretty mad alright, and he may be coming after me again, but I'll be ready for him. In the meantime, while he's coming, I'd like to get in more licks for Number One.[6]

In our secular and modern age, Cash's talk about the devil can seem a bit florid and excessive—too spooky, superstitious, and fundamentalist. Ratings for *The Johnny Cash Show* did take a hit, as predicted by the show runners, after Cash read his statement. And it's not hard to imagine why. Many of us, even devout Christians, just don't take the devil seriously anymore.

For years, I was one of these skeptical Christians who didn't have much use for the devil. But you know who caused me to start taking the devil more seriously? Addicts and inmates, two groups Johnny Cash knew very well. As Marty Stuart, a longtime friend of Cash, observed, Cash didn't fear much in the world, but he feared "the dark force of Satan." Stuart elaborates: "John fully understood the power of the dark force. He'd be on his knees with a Bible in his hands, trying to cope with his demons."[7]

My experiences teaching the Bible study in the prison and walking alongside friends struggling with addiction at our mission church Freedom Fellowship caused a revolution in my own spiritual worldview.[8] I don't really care how you think about the devil, but the choice between Jesus and the Lord of the Flies is real. Minute by minute, day by day, we make a choice between light and darkness, between life and death. Johnny Cash had to keep facing and making this choice his entire life. Even when sober, he still missed the drugs. The demons were still haunting. The flies were still buzzing.

———

No song recorded by Johnny Cash so dramatically captures this choice between God and the devil in the life of an addict than "Sunday Mornin' Coming Down," written by Kris Kristofferson. After Kristofferson finished the song, he wanted Cash to record it. And while the song perfectly captured Cash's own struggles, Kristofferson wrote it to describe his own battle with substance use. "That was probably the most autobiographical song I'd written at the time," shared Kristofferson. "I was thinking about losing my family and living in a condemned building in Nashville."[9]

Cash didn't immediately respond to Kristofferson's request to cover his song. "Sunday Mornin' Coming Down" was first recorded by Ray Stevens, and as Cash listened to the lyrics, he identified with the man in the song. "It didn't hit me until one day when I was at home and out by the lake and I realized how far I had come from the days when I felt like the man in the song . . . so empty and alone," reflected Cash. "All of a sudden the lines of the song started running through my head and I realized I could identify with every one of them."[10]

In "Sunday Mornin' Coming Down," a man wakes up with a hangover, headache pounding, on Sunday morning. After drinking a beer for breakfast, he finds a dirty shirt to put on and stumbles down the stairs. In a foul mood, the man walks through the neighborhood. Soon he's interrupted by sights, sounds, and smells of family and faith: the smell of fried chicken from a home gathered around Sunday lunch, the sight of a father pushing his daughter on a swing in a park, and the sound of hymns coming from a church building. As Sunday morning comes crashing down upon the man—all the sights, smells, and sounds of love and community—he faces the emptiness of his life. The singer finds himself lost and alone. And the prayer he offers up to the Lord is the self-destructive petition of all addicts. He wants to get stoned again to escape it all:

On a Sunday morning sidewalk
I'm wishing Lord that I was stoned
'Cause there's something in a Sunday
That makes a body feel alone.

The repeated reference to getting "stoned" in the chorus of "Sunday Mornin' Coming Down" was controversial. Such an overt reference to the drug culture shocked the pious sensibilities of the day. Before Cash performed the song on *The Johnny Cash Show*, a worried TV rep wanted the lyric "wishing Lord that I was stoned" changed to "wishing Lord that I was home." Cash stuck to the original.

"Sunday Mornin' Coming Down" went on to become an iconic Cash standard. The Man in Black, once again, was expressing solidarity with and empathy for the outcasts—this time for every person who had ever struggled with substance use and addiction. And much of this solidarity flowed out of Cash's own pain and failures.

———

The decade between 1957, when Cash first took that little white pill, and 1967, when his divorce to Vivian was finalized, were the darkest, most traumatic years of Cash's life. It's a miracle that he survived.

The year 1968 would prove to be Cash's turning point, spiritually, relationally, and artistically. Artistically, it was the year of the legendary *At Folsom Prison* concert, the performance that transformed Cash's career and launched him into superstardom. Relationally, Cash proposed to June Carter onstage at a concert. June said yes, and the two would remain married until June's death in 2003.

This love affair saved Cash's life. Yet June knew the risks she was taking in falling in love with and marrying such a dark and troubled man. She captured that blend of passion and danger in "Ring of Fire," the song she wrote about her love affair with Cash. As June shared, "I knew that from first looking at him that his hurt was as great as mine. . . . I stepped up to feel the fire and there is no way to be in that kind of hell, no way to extinguish a flame that burns, burns, burns."[11] But by all accounts, June did cool the hurt in Johnny. As John Carter Cash observed about his mother and father, "She cleared his spirit so many times of the dust and darkness, the anger and pain that often engulfed his life. He knew inside—though at times he obviously forgot—that she was more than he deserved, that she was his only by some grace God had provided him."[12]

Spiritually, 1968 was also the year Cash began pulling back from the abyss, fighting back against his addiction. Over the years, Cash told three stories that helped bring about the spiritual awakening that led him back into the light.

The first story was about Sheriff Ralph Jones in Lafayette, Georgia. Sheriff Jones arrested Cash for public drunkenness, and Cash spent the night in jail to sober up. In the morning, Cash was released from his cell and taken to see Sheriff Jones. "I've followed your career for over ten years," said the sheriff. "My wife and I have every record you've ever made. We love you. We've always loved you." The sheriff placed the drugs he had confiscated from Cash the night before on the counter, along with his money and personal items. No charges. Cash could take his drugs and leave.

Cash was confused. "But I don't understand why you're giving me the dope back," Cash said. "It's illegal."

"Right, it's illegal," Sheriff Jones replied. "It would be a sin and a crime for you to kill yourself, too. And that's exactly what those pills are doing to you."[13]

The sheriff's speech and actions both touched and rattled Cash. The Bible talks about God turning sinners over to a depraved mind, to let the consequences of our actions serve as their own punishment. That's what Sheriff Ralph Jones did with Johnny Cash that day, and it proved to be an important goad in getting Cash to take a hard look at himself.

Biographer Robert Hilburn questions some of the factual details of the second story Cash told about turning his life around, but Cash's retelling says something about how he interpreted his life.

Shattered by the guilt over his divorce with Vivian, Cash drove to Nickajack Cave on the Tennessee River, north of Chattanooga, with suicidal thoughts. He wanted to climb deep into the cave system, so deep he'd lose his way and die somewhere in the darkness. When psychologists assess suicide risk, one of the things they look at is the lethality of the plan the person is contemplating. Crawling deep into a cave system, hoping to get lost, isn't a very lethal, risky plan. Still, Cash was thinking suicidal thoughts after this divorce, and his suicide plan perfectly matched the state of his soul. He just wanted to crawl into a hole and die. Literally.

So Cash parked his Jeep and crawled off into the maze of darkness. Eventually, the batteries of his flashlight died, and the light went out. Cash lay down in the darkness, waiting—or at least wishing—to die. "The absolute lack of light was appropriate," Cash later shared. "At that moment, I was as far from God as I have ever been."

Then something wholly unexpected happened. A feeling of utter peace and security flooded his heart, soul, and mind. There, deep in the darkness, God came to Johnny Cash. Or, rather, Cash realized that God had never left him. "I thought I'd left Him," Cash realized, "but He hadn't left me."[14] He crawled out of the cave and back into the light.

The third story, dramatized in the 2005 film *I Walk the Line*, starring Joaquin Phoenix and Reese Witherspoon, involved a tractor accident at Cash's home. He'd been a few days sober but found a stash of pills. Succumbing to temptation, he took a handful. High and looking for excitement, he began driving his tractor along the cliff overlooking the lake on his property. Seeking a thrill, he drove the tractor close to the edge of the cliff. He got too close, and the tractor tumbled over the side into the lake. He struggled in the freezing water and was about to drown. Fortunately, Braxton Dixon witnessed the accident and rescued Cash. The near-fatal accident prompted a strong, assertive response from June. With the help of her parents, Maybelle and Ezra Carter, June nursed Cash through his withdrawal symptoms and back to sobriety and health.

Newly sober and with the demons quieted, at least temporarily, Cash started producing some of his most explicitly spiritual work. He recorded *The Holy Land*, a gospel album inspired by a visit to Israel. Cash had carried around a tape recorder during his tour of Israel and used those sounds on the album. *The Holy Land* was a precursor of the most ambitious project of Cash's career, *The Gospel Road*, a full-length movie using story and song to tell about the life of Jesus. During the filming, Cash was rebaptized in the Jordan River. He commenced writing a biography about the life of the apostle Paul, entitled *Man in White*. During these years, Cash formed a friendship with Billy Graham and began performing at Graham's popular crusades. And it was during this time that Cash felt called to read his statement about God and the devil to a national TV audience.

Cash saw much of this explicitly religious output as fulfilling his promise to his brother Jack—to be the preacher that Jack was never able to be. During the 1970s, Cash was very much an overt evangelist. But the deeper reason behind this season of spiritual outpouring was simple gratitude, an expression of thanksgiving and praise to the God who had saved him and rescued his life from the pit. Johnny Cash had been resurrected from the dead. And he was grateful.

Some hard times were still to come. *The Johnny Cash Show* was canceled in 1971. And the eighties would be Cash's "lost decade."

His popularity waned. In 1986, after a twenty-six-year partnership, Columbia Records dropped Cash from the label. And the drugs came creeping back.

Still, Cash never descended back into the madness that had characterized the early years. His marriage to June and his relationship with God formed a tether of love that wouldn't let him go. Cash continued to struggle, but God's grace helped him hold on. As Cash once shared, "The Master of Life's been good to me. He has given me strength to face past illnesses, and victory in the face of defeat. He has given me life and joy where others saw oblivion. He has given me a new purpose to live for, new services to render, and old wounds to heal."[15]

—

In our post-Christian world, it is increasingly unfashionable to share a gospel that emphasizes the forgiveness of sins. No one nowadays likes to be told they are a sinner in need of grace. No one is interested in hearing that Jesus died for their sins. When we think of Jesus, we like to think of him as a hero of justice, speaking truth to the powers that be, agitating for social change. At most, Jesus is an inspiring moral figure we aspire to emulate and follow. The notion that "Jesus died on the cross to save you from your sins" seems dated, old-fashioned, and a retreat back into a religious fundamentalism we are happy to leave behind.

But this is also the gospel according to Johnny Cash. Cash was a sinner, and he knew it. And if you spend any time at all, as I do each week, walking alongside the incarcerated and those struggling with addiction, you know there are people who struggle with guilt and need to hear a message of grace. I work with people who have hurt others, often in ways that cannot be easily, if ever, healed or mended. The burden of shame, guilt, and self-loathing from the sins they have committed is more than they can bear. They are broken and defeated and can't get up.

But over and over again, the gospel revives, redeems, rescues, restores, and resurrects my friends behind bars and those, like Cash, who have fallen off the wagon. Time and time again, we revisit the question and answer from Ezekiel 37, which recounts the vision of the Valley of Dry Bones. The prophet Ezekiel stands in the middle of a valley filled with skeletons. And the Lord asks, "Ezekiel, can these bones come back to life again?" If you've ever been a skeleton in the Valley of Dry Bones, that's the most important question of your life. Can I come back to life again? Is there grace, even for me? A new start? A new life? Can dead things—can I—come back to life again? God answers God's own question in Ezekiel by knitting the bones back together again and breathing life back into them.

Cash was once asked in an interview how he had survived his years of addiction. What had caused him to give up drugs? What had saved him? He had a simple, one-word answer: "God."[16]

Yes, by the loving grace of God, dead things can come back to life again. The grace that saved Johnny Cash is the grace that saves you and me. There is freedom and mercy for everyone—even for those stoned on Sunday morning.

PART 3

NATION AND NOSTALGIA

The Nazis marched through the dark night. They carried torches and chanted the chilling refrain, "Blood and soil! Blood and soil!" They gave the "Heil Hitler" salute. They proudly displayed the swastika. And one of them was spotted wearing a Johnny Cash T-shirt.

This wasn't Hitler's Germany in the 1930s and '40s. This was America in 2017. White separatists, supremacists, and nationalists had gathered in Charlottesville, Virginia, to protest the removal of the statue of Confederate general Robert E. Lee. Various neo-Nazi, Ku Klux Klan, and neo-Confederate groups had responded to the call to demonstrate against the removal of the statue and other Confederate monuments across the city. On the evening of August 11, a group of white nationalists carried torches on a march through the campus of the University of Virginia, the school founded by Thomas Jefferson. During the march, they chanted Nazi and white supremacist slogans such as "Jews will not replace us" and "Blood and soil!"

American news and social media flooded viewers' screens with pictures and videos of the Unite the Right rally, including the video of a neo-Nazi wearing a Johnny Cash T-shirt. The association of Johnny Cash with a hate-filled, white-supremacist protest drew a sharp and public rebuke from the Cash family. Rosanne Cash posted a passionate note on her Facebook page on behalf of herself and the other Cash children. Under the heading "A message from the children of Johnny Cash," Rosanne wrote, "We were alerted to a video of a young man in Charlottesville, a self-proclaimed neo-Nazi, spewing hatred and bile. He was wearing a t-shirt emblazoned with the name of Johnny Cash, our father. We were sickened by the association." Rosanne went on to describe her father and what he stood for:

> Johnny Cash was a man whose heart beat with the rhythm of love and social justice. He received humanitarian awards from, among others, the Jewish National Fund, B'nai Brith, and the United Nations. He championed the rights of Native Americans, protested the war in Vietnam, was a voice for the poor, the struggling and the disenfranchised, and an advocate for the rights of prisoners. . . . His pacifism and inclusive patriotism were two of his most defining characteristics. He would be horrified at even a casual use of his name or image for an idea or a cause founded in persecution and hatred. . . .
>
> Our dad told each of us, over and over throughout our lives, "Children, you can choose love or hate. I choose love." . . .

To any who claim supremacy over other human beings, to any who believe in racial or religious hierarchy: we are not you. Our father, as a person, icon, or symbol, is not you. We ask that the Cash name be kept far away from destructive and hateful ideology.

We Choose Love.[1]

——

Johnny Cash was a patriot, and he loved America. When you think of the music of the Man in Black, you mostly think of the music Rosanne Cash pointed to, the music where Cash speaks up for "the poor, the struggling and the disenfranchised." But Johnny Cash also sang a great deal about America. For example, in 1972, Cash released the concept album *America: A 200-Year Salute in Story and Song*. Posing with the American flag on the cover, Cash extols and memorializes American history and heroes. He opens the album quoting the US Constitution and then running through a list of American heroes who have helped forge our "more perfect union": Columbus, De Soto, Lewis and Clark, Kit Carson, Daniel Boone, David Crockett, Eli Whitney, Sam Colt, Thomas Edison, Henry Ford, Orville and Wilbur Wright, and Paul Revere. Cash also mentions his grandfather in the list. After the patriotic roll call, Cash launches into a song about Paul Revere. Later in the album, he sings about the Battle of New Orleans and the Alamo. He reads the Gettysburg Address. And the album ends with a love song to America, "These Are My People."

But it's not just one concept album devoted to America leading up to the 1976 bicentennial. The albums of Johnny Cash are filled with proud, nostalgic music extolling the American nation, its history, and its people. All that to say, we can see how an American patriot, even if that person was a neo-Nazi, would be attracted to the music of Johnny Cash. The music of Johnny Cash is as American as apple pie.

And that creates tensions for the gospel according to Johnny Cash, seen in the confrontation between a neo-Nazi fan and the children of Johnny Cash. The patriotism displayed in the music of Johnny Cash makes his gospel vulnerable to distortion and misappropriation, in exactly the same way that patriotism and nationalism of all sorts can distort and twist the gospel. Nationalistic nostalgia can lead us into some dark, troubled waters.

A Nazi could end up wearing your T-shirt.

No song better captures this nostalgia in Cash's music than "Ragged Old Flag." The song comes from the 1974 album of the same title. On the cover, Cash points toward a torn, worn American flag, and he has a stern, chastising look, as if to say, "Look at what you've done to America!"

The spoken-word song "Ragged Old Flag" recounts a narrative of loss and decay. The narrator of the song sits down next to an old man in a town outside a courthouse that has seen better days. The flag flying above the courthouse is rough and tattered. The old-timer starts talking, recounting all the battles and conflicts that have literally and symbolically damaged the flag: Washington crossing the Delaware, Francis Scott Key at Fort McHenry, Andrew Jackson in the Battle of New Orleans, the stand at the Alamo, Chancellorsville and Shiloh during the Civil War, Flanders in World War I, and the fighting of World War II, Korea, and Vietnam. At the time the song was released, Vietnam was still raging, with flags being burned in the streets, and the old man talks about how the flag was being damaged by the protests. The damage done to the flag by Watergate also gets an indirect mention in a reference to a government that has scandalized the nation. The song ends with the old man sharing how, despite its rough appearance flying over the courthouse, he's proud to brag over the "ragged old flag":

> So we raise her up every morning
> We take her down every night
> We don't let her touch the ground and we fold her up right
> On second thought, I do like to brag
> 'Cause I'm mighty proud of that ragged old flag.

The nostalgic temptation in a song like "Ragged Old Flag" is in its image of loss and decay. The flag—and the nation it represents—has been damaged. The assumption behind the song is that there was a time when the flag was pristine and new, or at least better off than it is now. We nostalgically look back at a time when America was good, great, and prosperous. Today, by contrast, America is broken, weak, and ragged.

The problem with this "narrative of injury" is that it conjures up feelings of resentment.[2] Looking upon a damaged America, we peer anxiously across the political aisle, our backyard fences, and our national borders, searching for the culprits, the people who are hurting America. The image of the ragged old flag—a damaged

America—creates suspicion and paranoia, and that fear breeds intolerance and hate. That's how flag-waving nostalgia provides the fuel for a torch-lit march where neo-Nazis chant, "Blood and soil!"

———

The far right isn't the only group tempted by nostalgia in American politics. Liberals have their own nostalgic tendencies. As Yuval Levin describes in his book *The Fractured Republic*, the American Left and Right are both trapped by a politics of nostalgia. Both liberals and conservatives look back at the post–World War II decades as a lost golden era that we need to restore and recover. Both Democrats and Republicans love to tell stories of this golden era, trying in their own ways to evoke a "ragged old flag" nostalgia to fuel their political projects and get-out-the-vote efforts during elections. The curiosity, according to Levin, is that both Republicans and Democrats hark back to the same era to evoke nostalgia; they just grab different pieces of the larger picture.

The decades after World War II were a time of great prosperity, which is why both Democrats and Republicans look back upon that period so fondly. They have in mind idyllic images of small towns and the green lawns of peaceful American suburbs. Of course, these images conveniently ignore the plight of black Americans and the *Father Knows Best* gender roles. Not everything was perfect. But the nostalgic imagery of political campaigns tells us that those were the good ol' days.

As Levin recounts, those years of prosperity after World War II were characterized by two great consolidations, one economic and the other cultural. Economically, America shifted its wartime energies into domestic production, creating the manufacturing boom upon which liberals look back so fondly. This was the era when labor unions were powerful and a blue-collar factory worker could earn a living wage and retire with a pension. Recollections of a time when the American dream was accessible to the blue-collar worker, as Dad lugged his lunch pail to the factory, are the stories Democrats love to tell at their national conventions.

Since that time, the economic forces of globalization and technology have drastically altered the American economy. "Made in America" became "Made in China" as manufacturing jobs moved overseas. Detroit and other hubs of American industry have struggled. Without good factory jobs, the region described as the nation's Rust Belt became overrun with methamphetamine and opioid use. Now a high-school diploma no longer guarantees a reliable path into the middle class. The economic consolidation of the post–World War II years has vanished.

Along with economic consolidation, the postwar years were also characterized by a cultural consolidation. This was the era of *Father Knows Best* and *Leave It to Beaver.* Culturally, America was more uniform in beliefs, values, worldview, and aspirations. America was white and Protestant. Gender roles were traditional, and sexual ethics were conservative. These are the stories that Republicans tell.

But that cultural consensus was lost during the social upheaval of the 1960s. The birth control pill was approved by the Food and Drug Administration in 1960. Civil rights legislation passed. Immigration shifted away from Western Europe. Church attendance began to fall. Culturally and demographically, America became more diverse and pluralistic. When conservatives speak of restoring a "Christian nation," they tell nostalgic stories of the pre-1960s cultural consensus—a golden era of solid, traditional family values.

In sum, argues Levin, both Republicans and Democrats are hopelessly mired in nostalgia. Both parties want to "make America great again," each in their own way. Democrats, given their historical association with labor unions, seek to restore the lost prosperity of America's working class.[3] Republicans, by contrast, seek to restore the values of a lost "Christian nation."

The trouble with this nostalgia-driven politics, Levin points out, is that neither golden era is coming back. Economically, the free-market forces of globalization prevent America from ever returning to our golden age of manufacturing. And culturally and demographically, the trends toward secularism and pluralism march steadily on. Nostalgic stories won't provide practical solutions for modern problems. True, the center isn't holding, but the answers we are looking for aren't going to be found by jumping into a time machine to go back to the 1950s. The world has changed. There is no going back. We have to look forward to find new, fresh solutions to our problems. Wave the ragged old flag as much as you want, but nostalgia is a dead end—for both political parties.

But most importantly, nostalgia has a bigger problem. As we've noted, nostalgia creates a politics of resentment. Nostalgia is doubly toxic. Stories of the good ol' days cannot provide us with practical, modern solutions. And as we spin our wheels, the nostalgia tempts us to hunt down and scapegoat the people who we think are damaging America. Things get worse, we start blaming each other, and then we tear each other to pieces.

We can keep the gospel according to Johnny Cash free from the temptations of patriotic nostalgia by focusing on his Man in Black solidarity. This is how we keep his image off the T-shirts of neo-Nazis chanting "Blood and soil!" The music of Johnny Cash is at its best, artistically and theologically, when he's singing about the people the American dream has left behind. When Cash sings, "These are my people" in his love song to America, we keep in view his advocacy for Native Americans, the prisoners cheering in Folsom and San Quentin, the Great Depression famers in Arkansas, the African American artists he invited on *The Johnny Cash Show*, and the alcoholic from "Sunday Mornin' Coming Down." These are the people of Johnny Cash's America. These are the Americans welcomed by what Rosanne Cash described as her father's "inclusive patriotism."

For us to avoid the trap of nostalgia, the songs we sing about America must be complicated and often critical. Such criticism is an expression of love and an act of patriotism. My favorite lyric in this regard comes from a little-known song written by Cash, "All God's Children Ain't Free," from his album *Orange Blossom Special*:

I'd sing more about more of this land
but all God's children ain't free.

Cash sang a lot about America, and he confessed to wanting to sing even more, but he also saw the darkness at work in his nation and its history. Here in America, many remain in bondage. Never forget those bitter tears. All God's children ain't free.

To be sure, Cash struggled to thread the needle here, in how to both love and criticize America. An example of this tension was on display when President Richard Nixon invited Cash to perform at the White House. Cash so respected the office of the president that he was honored to accept the invitation, much to the dismay of his fans on the political left. But there was also a snag. The Nixon administration asked Cash to perform two songs, both of which Cash found problematic. The first was "Okie from Muskogee" by Merle Haggard, a song that took shots at American youth, their anti-war sentiments and their counterculture. The second song was "Welfare Cadillac," a song Cash later described as "a lightning rod . . . for anti-black sentiment."[4] Cash refused to perform either song, telling the White House staffers that the president would get the same songs he did for prisoners and everyone else. And Cash went even further. He sang "What Is Truth?" a song he wrote expressing solidarity with American youth, especially their antiwar sentiments. *Rolling Stone* described "What Is Truth?" as "a country & western 'Times They Are a-Changin,'" referring to Bob Dylan's protest song. Nixon seemed to have gotten the point. "One thing I've learned about Johnny Cash," the president declared at the White House concert, "is that you don't tell him what to sing."

But still, isn't there some tension and even contradiction between praising Christopher Columbus at the start of *America* and the protest songs we listen to on *Bitter Tears*? Yes, there is, and I don't want to suggest that Cash himself fully reconciled his political inconsistencies. But Cash's music would be hopelessly vulnerable to patriotic nostalgia if *At Folsom Prison* and *Bitter Tears* didn't exist. Consequently, the *existence* of this tension and contradiction means we're on the right track. Our capacity for prophetic critique flows out of this conflict—the gap between national aspiration and national failure, between national pride and national guilt. When this conflict is lost, when we're waving flags in the face of those weeping bitter tears, we lose what Walter Brueggemann has called "the prophetic imagination," the ability to imagine our nation standing under the judgment of God, the imagination that God can be *against* us. To be sure, this will be harder or easier depending upon how you feel about America, but cultivating a capacity for prophetic critique is the task of every Christian, especially when you live in a nation you are proud of and grateful for. As Ralph Gleason wrote of Cash's political witness during the tumultuous years of Nixon, race riots, and Vietnam: "He's struggling. He's not perfect, but he's trying. He loves this country but he's trying to keep that from meaning he hates some other."[5]

In our own troubled, polarized political climate, none of us are perfect, and most of us are struggling. Like Johnny Cash, a lot of us are trying to love our country without that meaning we have to hate somebody else. We are grateful for our freedoms, but we are also crying out for "a more perfect union." In the end, I think Cash himself summed it up best: we'd "sing more about more of this land, but all God's children ain't free."

CHAPTER 12

"DRIVE ON"

Johnny Cash stood before a packed house at Madison Square Garden in 1969 while the Vietnam War was raging. At the peak of his popularity, the Man in Black was being thrust more than ever into the public eye. Reporters wanted Cash on the record about the war. Where did he stand? Was he for the war in Vietnam or against it? Was the Man in Black a hawk or a dove?

Standing before the New York audience, Cash gave his answer. Cash shared about performing for the troops at the Long Binh military base, near Saigon. Hearing about the show, a friend had confronted Cash with the question "That makes you a hawk, doesn't it?" Cash objected to the label and said to the Madison Square audience, "No, that doesn't make me a hawk, but when you watch the helicopters bringing in the wounded, that might make you a dove with claws."[1] The crowd cheered the line, and Cash launched into a song written by Ed McCurdy, "Last Night I Had the Strangest Dream," a song about ending war.

To some, a dove with claws is an attractive image, an attempt to find a proper balance between peace and aggression, not dissimilar to Jesus's recommendation to his followers, "Be shrewd as serpents, and innocent as doves" (Matthew 10:16). But there's also something contradictory about the image. It might even be a cop-out, a timid way of trying to have your cake and eat it, too. It's not a bad strategy if you're trying to avoid controversy—especially if you're trying to sell records.

In Cash's defense, I expect most Christians, at least of my acquaintance, if given the choice between "dove" or "hawk," would try to resist that either/or, to land where Cash landed, a "dove with claws." On the one hand, as followers of the Prince of Peace, we're called to be doves in the world. "Blessed are the peacemakers," Jesus said, "for they will be called children of God" (Matthew 5:9). We pray and work toward the world envisioned in Isaiah 2:4:

> They will beat their swords into plowshares
> > and their spears into pruning hooks.
> Nation will not take up sword against nation,
> > nor will they train for war anymore.

But on the other hand, evil exists, and many feel morally compelled to resist it, with force if necessary, to protect the weak and the innocent. We are not hawks, but we're not quite doves either. We find ourselves caught in the middle.

My point here isn't theological, political, or ethical. I'm not trying to make an argument for or against pacifism, an argument for or against Christians using force to face evil in the world. My point is that we're psychologically drawn to the "dove with claws" position.

It might be a contradiction, but it's not a cop-out. Issues related to war and peace are some of the most vexing questions facing Christians. The church has been split on the issue for two thousand years, and it remains hotly debated. In their Facebook note after the Unite the Right rally in Virginia, Rosanne Cash and her siblings described their father as a pacifist. If so, it was a restless, complicated, nuanced pacifism, a dove that was tempted to grow some claws.

———

Pacifism is unconditional obedience to Jesus's enemy-love commands in the Sermon on the Mount: "You have heard that it was said, 'Eye for eye, and tooth for tooth.' But I tell you, do not resist an evil person. If anyone slaps you on the right cheek, turn to them the other cheek also. You have heard that it was said, 'Love your neighbor and hate your enemy.' But I tell you, love your enemies and pray for those who persecute you, that you may be children of your Father in heaven" (Matt 5:38, 43–44a). Christians committed to unconditional nonviolence find it impossible to attach "claws" to Jesus's instructions. Love, they argue, doesn't have claws.

Yet the response is that the use of force against the violent and evil isn't motivated by any hatred of the enemy but is, instead, our attempt to love the victims of the world. To make this point, Jimmy Carter would frequently quote Reinhold Niebuhr: "The sad duty of politics is to establish justice in a sinful world."[2] In the language of Paul in Romans 13, governments have been established by God to use the sword to limit the impact of evil on the world: "For the one in authority is God's servant for your good. But if you do wrong, be afraid, for rulers do not bear the sword for no reason. They are God's servants, agents of wrath to bring punishment on the wrongdoer" (v. 4). The debate within Christianity rages about whether Christians, despite Jesus's teachings in the Sermon on the Mount, must share the burden of the "sad duty" described in Romans 13. I'm not going to settle that question for you, but I do believe the *sadness* of the duty points us toward the gospel according to Johnny Cash.

Many Christians are uneasy about trying to give specific, universal rules for how to navigate the hotly contested ethical issues regarding the use of force in the world. But what I think the gospel demands that we all agree on is that violence is always, always tragic. Violence always represents a failure. Maybe, in the face of evil, we think it's a necessary failure, but it's a failure nonetheless. It might be a duty, but it's a sad duty. Any justice we feel obligated to create with the sword falls eternally short of the kingdom of God, where nations no longer train for war.

So the gospel according to Johnny Cash is this: violence is always tragic. Christians can never cheer, applaud, or baptize a nation's use of violence and force. Such uses are only and always tragedies, sad duties that must be grieved and mourned—and most importantly, circumscribed and limited.

Here, perhaps, is room for common ground between Christian pacifists and Christians who believe war can be justified. If Christians fully and properly grieved and mourned the tragic failure of violence, there would be much less of it in the world. If we stopped cheering and applauding violence, our nations would be slower in resorting to the sword and more willing to pursue other means of conflict-resolution. If we wept instead of cheered over the deaths of our enemies, our nations would be quicker to beat their swords into plowshares.

———

This is where the peace witness of Johnny Cash is at its gospel best—when he sings about the pain, suffering, and tragedy of war, especially the way war damages the soldier and the soldier's family. As always, the gospel according to Johnny Cash finds its natural home in the intimate, human spaces of heartache, brokenness, and loss. Here's how Rodney Clapp describes it:

> [Cash] was proud of his own military service and often commemorated American military battles in song. Yet even in the realm of heroic warfare, Cash can evidence ambivalence. His 1972 track "The Big Battle" receives little comment but is a remarkable piece of folkloric but deromanticizing songwriting. It's the closest thing Cash ever wrote to an outright antiwar song. In it, a young Civil War solider hears the shooting fade out and is ready to disarm, thinking the conflict is done. His commanding officer is more seasoned and rebukes the younger solider. The physical warfare may be done, but the "big battle" is yet to come and will span over decades. It will, says the officer, "rage in the bosom of mother and sweetheart and wife / Brother and sister and daughter will grieve for the rest of their lives." . . . Dropping gun and saber, [the young solider] reports himself ready for the real battle of life after the profound destruction of warfare.[3]

The gospel according to Johnny Cash points us toward the "big battle"—toward the mothers, wives, sweethearts, brothers, sisters, and daughters who grieve for the rest of their lives. Cash's music describes the emotional and spiritual damage caused by the sword, the "profound destruction of warfare."

Cash wrote many songs about the "big battle." One is the spoken-word song "Route No. 1, Box 144," about a young farm boy—a normal, average boy, no one special. He falls in love and marries his sweetheart. They move into a small house at Route No. 1, Box 144. The boy is called off to war and is killed. The telegram informing his bride of his death shows up in the mailbox. And then later, his body arrives. The boy's death doesn't make the news or any headlines. He is just one more anonymous casualty of war, one name in a long list of names. But at the address Route No. 1, Box 144, the news is world shattering and catastrophic.

"Route No. 1, Box 144" is a powerful example of the "big battle"—how the calculus of loss can be truly measured only in the suffering of those who grieve. We can't begin to take in the full scope of the tragedy of war until we attend to the private and particular. The weight of pain at a particular address, with a particular family is beyond calculation. The gospel according to Johnny Cash finds its proper place in telling us that story. Listen to the wails of grief coming from behind the door at Route No. 1, Box 144.

My favorite example of Cash singing about the "big battle" is his song "Drive On," which appeared on Cash's first album with Rick Rubin, *American Recordings*. Cash explained the origin of the song in a 1997 VH1 special he recorded with Willie Nelson. The show was at an intimate venue, where a small audience saw the two elderly icons of country, rock 'n' roll, folk, and outlaw music swap songs, accompanying themselves on their acoustic guitars.

Before playing "Drive On," Cash explained that at one point, June and he had been doing a lot of reading about the Vietnam War. Cash described how soldiers out on patrol would get shot and drop dead. Their buddies would have "no time to stop and grieve them; you might get shot," Cash explained. "So they'd say, 'Drive on, it don't mean nothing'—when it meant everything."[4] He sang:

> It was a slow walk in a sad rain
> And nobody tried to be John Wayne
> I came home, but Tex did not
> And I can't talk about the hit he got.
>
> Drive on, it don't mean nothin'.

It's a gut-wrenching description of the psychological trauma war inflicts upon soldiers—how a solider would have to numb himself to the death of a friend ("it don't mean nothin'") in order to cope and stay alive.

Studies estimate that 30 percent of Vietnam War veterans suffered from PTSD.[5] A more recent study of Gulf War veterans, a 2015 review published in the *Journal of Anxiety Disorders*, found that 23 percent suffered from PTSD.[6] Those rates are three to five times higher than for the general population. At the heart of PTSD are "intrusive" symptoms, when the traumatic event invades consciousness, causing the person to relive or re-experience the trauma. Intrusive symptoms include unwanted traumatic memories, flashbacks, nightmares, and extreme reactions to reminders of and triggers associated with the traumatic event. A debilitating mental illness, PTSD is associated with addiction, domestic violence, depression, psychosis, and suicide. When Johnny Cash sang about war, he was singing for the veterans fighting this "big battle," the men and women carrying the hidden, psychic scars of war.

"Drive On" is vintage Johnny Cash, and when it comes to him speaking prophetically about the human tragedy of war, the VH1 performance is one of his finest moments. Furthermore, the contrast with Willie Nelson, along with the effect upon the audience, is profound. Michael Streissguth, in his biography of Cash, describes the impact of the song's performance. Streissguth notes how the audience had warmed to Nelson over Cash as Willie ripped through his greatest hits, from "Crazy" to "Funny How Time Slips Away." Cash, by contrast, avoided "I Walk the Line" and "Folsom Prison Blues," preferring to sing songs that were meaningful to him but largely unknown to the audience. After exchanging songs back and forth, Cash then paused to share the story of "Drive On" before launching into his song of trauma, grief, and loss. The contrast with Nelson's sentimental love songs was stark, and Streissguth summarizes its effect upon the audience:

> [By singing "Drive On," Cash] summarily reminded the audience of his towering authority, over Nelson and over all comers. The utter seriousness of war and desperation trumped Nelson's pain of love and heartbreak, stilling the audience and delivering the show and its audience back to Cash's bosom. Nelson followed with his honky-tonk classic "Me and Paul," but in the wake of "Drive On," it was like water after wine.[7]

PART 4

SUFFERING AND SALVATION

CHAPTER 13

"DELIA'S GONE"

Commercially, the 1980s were not very good to Johnny Cash, often described as his "lost decade." Cash dominated the airwaves during the fifties, sixties, and seventies. It was an amazing streak of popularity and commercial success. But no artist can sustain that level of cultural relevance, not for an entire lifetime. Each successive generation pushes the sounds and sensibilities of an artist further into the past. In the eighties, Cash was universally revered, a cultural icon, a senior statesman of country music. But that didn't mean anyone was buying his records.

And truth be told, there wasn't much to listen to. Cash kept putting out records in the eighties, but none of them made you sit up and take notice the way "Folsom Prison Blues" once did. Cash's music was monotonous and unremarkable. Can you name a single Cash hit from the eighties? A single album of note?

In addition, the sinister edge to Cash's persona—the Man in Black cussing and singing about murder in front of roaring prison inmates—had long been replaced by the Christian family man. No longer a symbol of protest and the counterculture, Cash had acquired a tamed and institutionalized image.

Things reached their low point in 1986. On July 16, readers of the *Tennessean* awoke to this headline: "Man in Black without a Label." Columbia Records had been worried for some time about Cash's declining record sales. They finally pulled the trigger and dropped him from the label. Reporting on the rumors circulating around Music City, the story in the *Tennessean* read, "Johnny Cash is without a country music label. The Country Music Hall of Fame member who is arguably the most legendary star in country music has been with Columbia Records since 1958, but sources at the company say his contract will not be renewed."[1] Cash was humiliated. He was eventually picked up by Mercury Records, but his records sales continued to lag.

Another low point occurred in 1993, when Cash did a stint in Branson, Missouri, that mecca of nostalgia. Nothing quite signals the end of your cultural and artistic relevance as much as playing a set of greatest hits before busloads of octogenarians and families on vacation. Cash felt like he was being put out to pasture. The Branson vibe depressed him.

But the winds were starting to change for Johnny Cash. Before beginning the show in Branson, Cash had a few tour commitments, mainly playing small, five-hundred-seat club venues, a far cry from singing before thousands at Madison Square Garden. But at his performance at the Rhythm Café in Santa Ana, California, Cash met the man who would change his life. A burly, bearded, long-haired young man walked into the Rhythm Café dressing room and introduced himself to Cash. Cash reached out and shook hands with Rick Rubin.

It was an unlikely partnership and collaboration. Cash was a past-his-prime, best-years-behind-him, sixty-one-year-old country legend. Rubin was a scruffy, thirty-year-old producer of rap, hip-hop, punk, and heavy-metal bands. But Cash was out of options, and Rubin was looking for a challenge, an opportunity to work with a music legend whose best work seemed to be behind him. As Rubin shared about his motives in looking for and working with a washed-up music icon, "I wanted to see if I could help them do great work again."[2]

After their initial meeting and follow-up conversations, Cash visited Rubin's home and studio in Los Angeles. Rubin sat Cash down and began simply, asking Cash to play some of his favorite songs. Rubin listened as Cash sang, accompanying himself on his guitar. Cash played gospel songs, train songs, silly songs, and Western songs. That first session, Rubin searched for the soul of the Man in Black. He didn't even hit the record button.

During the second session, Rubin began to record, encouraging Cash when he heard a song that evoked the singer of the 1950s and '60s. One of those songs, a song that Cash had written four years earlier but hadn't yet recorded, was "Drive On."

And then Cash sang Rubin a murder ballad. That was their breakthrough.

———

On Christmas Eve 1900, Moses Houston shot and killed his lover, Delia Green. The murder of Delia Green in Savannah, Georgia, went on to become the subject of two folk ballads, "Delia" and "Delia's Gone." The sad story of a man shooting his lover was carried far and wide by traveling folk musicians. Artists including Bob Dylan and Pete Seeger introduced the murder of Delia Green to the wider public during the 1950s American folk revival.

The real-life Houston and Green were teenagers living in Yamacraw, the black section of Savannah. On the night of the murder, the lovers had a fight. At one point, Delia called Houston a "son of a bitch." An enraged Houston, who was drunk, pulled out a gun and shot Delia in the groin, killing her. Houston was convicted of Delia's murder but escaped the gallows, sentenced instead to life in prison.

Though inspired by the murder of Delia Green, the ballad "Delia's Gone" was widely interpreted and elaborated upon by folk singers, with no version exactly the same as another or exactly corresponding to the murder it was based on. The song that broke upon the American folk scene in the fifties is chillingly told from the perspective of the murderous lover, who shoots Delia not once, but twice. An early version of the ballad was entitled "One More Rounder Gone," and subsequent versions built the song around the chorus "Delia gone, one more round, Delia gone."[3]

Inspired by the folk artists, Cash recorded a traditional version of "Delia's Gone" on his 1962 album *The Sound of Johnny Cash*. But more than thirty years later, with Rick Rubin, Cash added some darker twists to the song, making the killer colder and more sociopathic. In Cash's 1962 version, the killer simply mentions shooting Delia twice, following the "One More Rounder Gone" tradition of the song. But in the Rick Rubin version, Cash has the jealous killer tying Delia to a chair and shooting her with a submachine gun. A submachine gun is an unlikely weapon for a domestic homicide, but it's a lyrical twist that amps up the lethality and the violence of the murder.

Like Moses Houston, the killer in the ballad is eventually sentenced to life in prison. Beyond the shocking violence of the song, the real pathos of "Delia's Gone" comes from how the killer is haunted by the ghost of the murdered Delia. Sitting alone in the darkness and silence of his cell, the killer can't sleep because he hears the spectral footsteps of Delia's ghost pattering around his bed.

When Cash played "Delia's Gone," it caught Rubin's attention. Biographer Robert Hilburn describes what caught Rubin's ear: "This was the tough, hard-edged side of Cash that Rubin wanted to hear, the side he felt had largely been missing from Cash's recordings since he became a symbol of American goodness and family in the 1970s."[4] As Rubin himself said about "Delia's Gone," he was looking for "the original Johnny Cash who loomed large and was surrounded by all this darkness, yet who still had vulnerability. I wanted, if you will, to take him back to the 'I shot a man in Reno just to watch him die' Man in Black, and 'Delia's Gone' did it perfectly. He kills a girl, and then is remorseful. I loved how the brutal act was followed by this haunted life."[5]

When Cash and Rubin released *American Recordings*, their first album together, the opening track was "Delia's Gone." In leading with a murder ballad, Rubin was sending a message: the Man in Black is back. As it turned out, Cash was so back and black that MTV refused to show the "Delia's Gone" music video with Kate Moss starring as Delia's corpse.

The album *American Recordings* went on to become a critical and commercial success, winning the 1995 Grammy for Best Contemporary Folk Album.

———

Of course, the gospel according to Johnny Cash is found in the "lost decade," in the sober family man of the 1980s. The Christian witness of Johnny Cash during those years was that of a recovering addict. But with the start of the Rick Rubin years, we are back to looking for the gospel in a murder ballad. And Rick Rubin put his finger on it when he described the killer in "Delia's Gone" as "haunted" by his crime. The ghost of Delia will not allow her killer to rest. Sin has left him permanently scarred.

This is the haunting we first heard in "Folsom Prison Blues," the regret of a cold-blooded killer singing the blues as he hears the lonesome whistle passing by. The violence—shooting a man in Reno just to watch him die—isn't romanticized. Our sins carry consequences. The killers in Cash's music end up in prison, haunted by ghosts, or swinging from the gallows. As Rodney Clapp observes, "Cash's songs depicting violence rarely idolized or glorified it. His doers of violence suffer remorse, torment, and imprisonment or execution as consequences of their actions."[6] Quentin Tarantino observes that in Cash's murder ballads, regret is the dominant theme: "Regret for the freedom lost. Regret for the non-life [the killer] faces. Regret for the road he chose. Regret for the life not lived, that only now does he realize was decent and noble. Regret for the violence inside of him, that he could have controlled, but which he let control him. Regret for the one moment of violence that took everything from him and cannot be taken back. And even the killer's regret for his victim. As the man who shot Delia twice tells his jailer."[7]

———

The church fathers describe sin as a wound. And for the most part, it's a self-inflicted wound. In many conservative, Evangelical churches, sin is mostly viewed as a mistake, "missing the mark" that causes the wrath of God to come raining down upon us. And no doubt, this crime-and-punishment view of sin is a part of the gospel according to Johnny Cash. As a sinner, Cash embraced grace when he moved out of the darkness of addiction and into the light.

But more and more, I've come to believe that the church fathers had the better view of sin. When I think of my own sin, I don't think much about judgment day and the wrath of God. I think about all the damage I've done to myself—all the self-inflicted wounds, from small scraps to huge, lacerating cuts upon my heart, conscience, and soul, day after day, year after year. Wound after wound after wound.

One day, I found myself sitting alone in the pews of an empty Catholic church. As I sat in the silence, all those self-inflicted wounds from over the years came flooding into my mind. Sad, haunting memories. Ghosts pattering around the pews. I hadn't sought the church for confession. But these were the memories that rushed in and filled my mind when I allowed myself to stop and sit in silence. Suddenly, and without warning, I found myself overwhelmed by my sin. It wasn't a fearful, wrath-of-God sort of experience; it was all sadness. I simply had an overwhelming sense of all the damage I'd done to myself, as well as to others—all the self-inflicted wounds, large and small, sprinkled across the years. The words of Psalm 38 came crashing down upon me:

> My guilt has overwhelmed me
>> like a burden too heavy to bear.
> My wounds fester and are loathsome
>> because of my sinful folly.
> (vv. 4–5)

Fortunately, most would consider my ghosts to be small potatoes. I've not murdered anybody. Unlike Delia's killer, I don't hear the ghostly footsteps of my victims in my bedroom. Still, I've damaged myself.

On Monday nights out at the prison, I spend time with men whose stories sound a lot like "Delia's Gone." The inmates are tough guys, and they work to keep that hard façade in front of each other during the class. But occasionally, when I'm alone with one of them, I get to see beneath the surface. I get to see the wounds, the sadness, and the ghosts. And the weight of guilt and shame is just crushing. I've held huge, tattooed men in my arms as their bodies heave with uncontrollable sobs that will not stop—wave upon wave of grief.

In moments like those, I glimpse the gospel according to Johnny Cash in a song like "Delia's Gone," that place where the terrible grace of God is visited upon us. This is the holy ground where our self-inflicted wounds are laid open and bare, where guilt and shame convulse us with drowning sorrow, bringing us to the threshold of repentance.

Grace comes to us in the suffering of sin. There is a sermon in the damage we have done to ourselves and to others. Pain becomes the doorway to salvation, and our tears are a bridge for the awful grace of God.

CHAPTER 14

"HURT"

March 14, 1998. There he was on the pages of *Billboard* magazine—the Man in Black giving the finger to the Nashville music establishment. You've likely seen the iconic image of Cash. It's a favorite for outlaw T-shirts and college dorm posters. It shows a snarling Johnny Cash giving the middle finger, that universal symbol saying "f— you," during a performance.

Ever since Columbia Records dropped him in 1986, Cash felt he'd been dismissed and ignored by the country music industry in Nashville. It took someone from outside the Music City establishment—namely, Rick Rubin—to give Cash the time and attention he'd deserved from a music producer. The Grammy for *American Recordings* proved that Cash still had good music in him. Nashville had made a mistake in putting him out to pasture. Plus, there were some industry murmurs about a hip-hop producer from California producing Cash. Rubin, it had been whispered, would do something to screw up Cash's sound and image.

Given those industry misgivings, Cash and Rubin felt vindicated by the success of *American Recordings*. But the country music establishment ignored the album, and the music didn't get much airplay on country radio stations. No doubt, Nashville was feeling a bit territorial about a California producer, known best for his work with LL Cool J, Run DMC, and the Beastie Boys, edging in on their market.

Not to be deterred, Cash and Rubin quickly followed up with a second album, *American Recordings II: Unchained*, which went on to become another critical and commercial success, eventually winning the 1998 Grammy for Best Country Album. That second Grammy, this time in the Nashville-dominated Country category, was even sweeter than the first. Rubin and Cash had gone up against the best music Nashville had to offer, and they had won.

Cash and Rubin were thrilled. Rubin, especially, wanted to do a victory lap at the expense of the Music City skeptics and naysayers, so he took out a full-page ad in the March 14, 1998, issue of *Billboard*, using the iconic picture of Cash flipping the bird to the camera. Cash wavered about using the photo but ultimately gave his blessing. The caption of the photo read, "American Recordings and Johnny Cash would like to acknowledge the Nashville music establishment and country radio for your support."

Message sent.

———

The famous photo of the Man in Black giving the middle finger came from the 1969 concert at San Quentin State Prison. It was taken by Jim Marshall, who also photographed the historic Folsom concert. The story behind the iconic "finger picture" is a bit murky.

The story Cash typically told involved the British film crew on hand at San Quentin to film the performance for a documentary. During the concert, Cash grew irritated with the members of the crew, who were getting in his way and blocking his view of the audience. Frustrated, he flipped them off. Jim Marshall snapped a picture, capturing the moment.

Jim Marshall, however, has a different memory of the shot. He recalls snapping the picture during the concert sound check. "John," Marshall recalls asking, "let's do one for the warden." Cash flipped him the bird, and Marshall took the picture.[1]

Many Cash fans, when they think of Cash being the Man in Black, think about the Johnny Cash of that photo. But if there was any meaning to be attached to his black attire, Cash gave his interpretation in the song "Man in Black." Wearing black was a sign of solidarity with the broken and beaten down. Yet, for many Cash fans, the Man in Black is an outlaw image—Johnny Cash as rebel and all-around badass.

The image does fit. People tend to forget that by starting out with Sun Records alongside Elvis and Jerry Lee Lewis, Cash began his career as a rock 'n' roll star. And on the road during those years, Cash contributed his fair share to establishing the image of the rock 'n' roll star as a drug-using, hotel-trashing, girl-chasing bad boy. In fact, Cash had trashed so many hotels in his life that he knew the price of every piece of furniture in a hotel room by heart.

Ever since the Jesus People movement, when Evangelical Christianity joined forces with the 1960s and '70s counterculture, there have been attempts to cast Jesus as the quintessential rebel and outsider. On his 1972 album *Only Visiting This Planet*, an album that gave birth to the contemporary Christian music industry, Larry Norman sings a song describing Jesus as "the outlaw." A famous wanted poster from the Jesus People that was circulated during the seventies read:

WANTED

JESUS CHRIST

ALIAS:

THE MESSIAH, THE SON OF GOD, KING OF KINGS, LORD OF LORDS, PRINCE OF PEACE, ETC.

Notorious leader of an underground liberation movement.

Wanted for the following charges:

- Practicing medicine, winemaking and food distribution without a license.
- Interfering with businessmen in the temple.
- Associating with known criminals, radicals, subversives, prostitutes and street people.
- Claiming to have the authority to make people into God's children.

APPEARANCE: Typical hippie type—long hair, beard, robe, sandals. Hangs around slum areas, few rich friends, often sneaks out into the desert.

BEWARE: This man is extremely dangerous. His insidiously inflammatory message is particularly dangerous to young people who haven't been taught to ignore him yet. He changes men and claims to set them free.

WARNING: HE IS STILL AT LARGE![2]

The Jesus-as-outlaw trend has continued. In an ever-evolving attempt to appeal to the young, churches routinely describe Jesus as a nonconformist and a rebel—Jesus as hippie or a saintly James Dean. Churches woo the young by marketing themselves as relevant, hip, and cool. Youth pastors sport tattoos. Church leaders drink and cuss. Rock concerts pass as worship. Just look around: Jesus and the church have become very cool, or at least they try hard to be.

To be sure, Jesus was a nonconformist, rebel, and outlaw. He was crucified, after all. And Christians are called to follow in the footsteps of their countercultural leader. As Paul declares in Romans 12:2, "Do not conform to the pattern of this world."

Yet in America today, there's nothing more conformist than being a nonconformist, nothing more predictable than being a rebel, and nothing more mainstream than being alternative. Much of this is due to how our consumerist culture sells us the image of being a rebel. We live in a world where you can buy designer jeans with holes already ripped for you, and "alternative" is a genre of very popular music. As Thomas Frank writes, "We consume not to fit in, but to prove, on the surface at least, that we are rock 'n' roll rebels, each one of us as rule-breaking and hierarchy-defying as our heroes of the 60s, who now pitch cars, shoes, and beer."[3] Here in America, all you need to be a rebel is a credit card.

So if we're going to be looking for rebellion in the gospel according to Johnny Cash, it needs to be the rebellion that truly and deeply subverts the norms of our society. That Johnny Cash flipping you off from the poster on the dorm room wall? He's not the Man in Black you're looking for.

———

If anyone knew how to package, market, and sell rebellion to America's youth, it was Rick Rubin. But the outlaw image wasn't what Rubin wanted to display on his albums with Cash. As Robert Hilburn describes, "Part of Rubin's genius was that he didn't simply portray Cash as a rebel. He wanted to break through the public image of Cash as a superhero by capturing his human side—the struggle and the pain and the grit."[4] This is the Man in Black Rubin was after: "When I asked artists what they admired about him, that's what they often mentioned—that vulnerable, hurt aspect, the man who wouldn't give up."[5] The culmination of this vision, bringing into view the pain and suffering of the Man in Black, the side of Cash that *hurt*, happened when Rubin suggested an unlikely song to Cash: "Hurt" by Trent Reznor of Nine Inch Nails.

Some covers of songs become more famous than the original recordings, and Johnny Cash was aware of this. For years, Cash watched Carl Perkins perform his song "Blue Suede Shoes," the song Elvis famously covered to the point of eclipsing the original. You can also make a good argument that Cash's cover of "Hurt" is more popular than the original. Readers of *Rolling Stone* have ranked Cash's performance of "Hurt" as the second-greatest cover of all time (second only to Jimmy Hendrix's cover of Bob Dylan's "All Along the Watchtower").[6] In fact, Cash's cover of "Hurt" was so authoritative that Reznor himself felt he had ceded the rights to the song. Recalling the first time he heard Cash sing his song, Reznor shared, "Tears started welling up. I realized it wasn't really my song anymore. It just gave me goose bumps up and down my spine. It's an unbelievably powerful piece of work."[7]

For what would be their fourth album, *American IV: The Man Comes Around*, Rubin was searching for songs that would create a potent combination of contemporary songwriting mixed with Cash's aged authority—poetry from a younger generation recited from the perspective of an older man, a man who has lived his life and looks back with regret, sorrow, and pain. Rubin had a collection of these songs he wanted to hear Cash sing. But of those songs, nothing stood out the way "Hurt" did.

Trouble was, Cash didn't seem interested. But after some encouragement from Rubin, he finally agreed to try the song. And the rest, as they say, was history.

—

Reznor wrote "Hurt" in the midst of depression and a heroin addiction. As Mikal Gilmore writes, "'Hurt' is the story of a man who suffers more for all the ways he makes others suffer. In fact, it is a song about an addict who looks unblinkingly at the worst truth he has ever encountered—the abyss of his own heart. . . . Cash knew this territory well. He had mapped it, ransacked it and even tried to crawl off and die inside its caves." In singing "Hurt," Gilmore goes on to say, Cash "was describing unsparingly what he had learned of himself in his darkest recesses."[8]

While Cash certainly did identify with the hurt an addict causes himself and those he loves, he also saw in "Hurt" themes of a larger, spiritual struggle. No doubt, addiction is a part of this struggle, but it also encompasses all the false gods and idols we pursue in life, all the vanity, pride, and selfishness. All of it, in the words of the song, is our "empire of dirt." Sung by an aging Cash looking back over his life, "Hurt" evokes the words of the preacher from Ecclesiastes: "Vanity of vanities, all is vanity."

This vanity is illustrated even more clearly in the music video Cash filmed to accompany the release of "Hurt." In the video, scenes of a young, vibrant Cash are juxtaposed with the elderly, feeble Cash, sitting alone at a banquet table filled with delicacies. Images of Cash strutting onstage cut away to images of the House of Cash, the museum Cash owned and ran to celebrate his career. The House of Cash had closed some years before and had fallen into a shocking state of disrepair. The images of the empty, dilapidated museum powerfully illustrate how quickly fame and success fade and deteriorate. Leaving no room to misunderstand his point, at the end of the video, Cash picks up a goblet of wine and pours it out upon the table. The gesture says it all.

Vanity of vanities, says the Man in Black, all is vanity.

———

But there's more in the song and video of "Hurt" than a reflection on the pride and vanity of humanity. Most listeners and viewers are struck by a profound sense of sadness and loss. Lyrically, the song describes how we eventually, if we live long enough, come to lose everyone we've ever loved. Loss after loss, we are slowly left all alone. The video includes multiple shots of June watching Johnny playing his guitar. Tears shimmer in her eyes. These tears are juxtaposed with images of Johnny and June when they were younger, happy, smiling, and walking arm in arm. Combined with the lyrics of loss, the images just rip your heart out. Many have said that "Hurt" is the saddest video they have ever seen. The emotional resonances of the video were so powerful that it was nominated for six awards, including Video of the Year, at the MTV Video Music Awards.

All told then, three emotional threads weave through "Hurt," lyrically and visually: regret, vanity, and loss. The references to addiction in "Hurt" highlight the regrets from Cash's life. As John Carter Cash describes the video of "Hurt," Cash "digs back through a painful past and reflects on the pains and the sufferings and hurts he lived and caused."[9] Most of this suffering was carried by the Cash children, Vivian, and June. Deeper still are the regrets that haunted Cash about Jack's death. What if he had done more to convince Jack to go fishing that day? As Rosanne Cash observed about her father, "He can't be read or understood out of the context of losing his brother. After that, he was driven by his grief."[10]

In addition to the regret is the vanity, being confronted in the face of death with the fleeting nature of success, wealth, and fame:

And you can have it all
My empire of dirt

As Jesus predicted, the treasures we lay up on earth are all eaten away by moths and rust. We come to the end only to realize, perhaps too late, that we've spent our lives building castles in the sand.

Lastly, there is loss. There are the tragic, catastrophic, unexpected losses. Cash experienced these during his life—the death of Jack and the tragic death of Luther Perkins, killed in a house fire in 1968. But "Hurt" especially evokes the losses that accumulate over time:

Everyone I know
Goes away in the end.

Drop by drop, funeral after funeral, everyone eventually, inevitably, goes away in the end.

As you might imagine, it's difficult to be both an outlaw and a saint, though Cash tried to pull it off his entire career. One minute he's cussing on the stage at Folsom Prison, the next he's singing a gospel song about Jesus. One minute he's flipping you the finger, the next he's quoting the Bible. That juxtaposition of light and darkness, murder and Jesus, is riveting and exhilarating, but it's also jarring and confusing. And it might also be incoherent and ultimately impossible. As my friend Mark Love has observed, the outlaw and saint were "conflicting images Cash tried to hold together. He cultivated both his image as an outlaw and a saint. He sang 'Folsom Prison Blues' and 'Rock of Ages,' trying to be simultaneously sinner and saint."[11] The problem with these dual images, as Mark goes on to say, is this: "This is a tough tension, however, around which to sustain an identity. The outlaw image tends to prevail." And for much of Cash's life, especially during the darkest days of his addiction, the outlaw image did prevail, with tragic results.

But with "Hurt," recorded at the end of Cash's life, the image undergoes a change. Rubin helped Cash shift from the image of the *outlaw* saint to the image of the *suffering* saint. As Mark says, with Rubin, "the outlaw/saint dichotomy had been replaced by something else, the sufferer/saint, and the result was more satisfying."[12] Rubin didn't want to feature Cash the rebel; he wanted to show the pain and vulnerability that had attracted so many to Cash's life and music. "Hurt" represents the culmination of that vision, Rubin's insight into the gospel according to Johnny Cash. This is a gospel not found in Jesus the "outlaw"—the cool, hip, relevant Jesus who cusses and flips you the finger—but the Jesus who, in the words of Isaiah 53, is the Man of Sorrows acquainted with grief. This is what "Hurt" gives us—the Man in Black as the Man of Sorrows. As John Carter Cash observed about his father, "My dad identified with the Old Testament character of Job, who lost all. Dad was also familiar with suffering. . . . Like Job, I believe Dad never cursed God, but rather came to accept his burden as best a human could."[13]

We're attracted to the image of the rebel because it makes us feel powerful and confident. But the gospel according to "Hurt" is that we are closest to God when we are at our weakest. Here we find the deep rebellion at the heart of the kingdom of God. Nothing attracts us to suffering. Nothing draws us to those places where we are broken, needy, and dependent. But that's exactly where grace comes to find us. God comes to us in our hurt.

In 2 Corinthians, the apostle Paul describes his hurt, a "thorn in his flesh" that is tormenting him. Paul prays for deliverance. This is the answer Paul receives:

> But [the Lord] said to me, "My grace is sufficient for you, for my power is made perfect in weakness." Therefore I will boast all the more gladly about my weaknesses, so that Christ's power may rest on me. That is why, for Christ's sake, I delight in weaknesses, in insults, in hardships, in persecutions, in difficulties. For when I am weak, then I am strong. (2 Cor 12:9–10)

That is the subversive gospel in Cash's "Hurt": the sufficiency of grace in our weakness, frailty, and suffering. True, this version of Johnny Cash might not be found on T-shirts or dorm-room posters. It's too radical for the radicals. We'd rather play the rebel and the hero. But grace comes to us in our weakness. That is the gospel in "Hurt." That is the Man in Black we are looking for.

CHAPTER 15

"THE MAN COMES AROUND"

One of the last songs Johnny Cash wrote, the greatest gospel song he would ever compose, began with a dream about the Queen of England.

Cash's health was deteriorating as *American IV: The Man Comes Around* was being recorded, the fourth album he would release with Rubin. Cash was so frail that, for some sessions, Rubin had to record him singing one line at a time, each part to be spliced together later. Cash's physical decline accelerated after the release of the album. June, his true love and soul mate, died unexpectedly in May 2003. June was younger and in better health than Johnny, so everyone expected him to go first. But June died following complications from heart valve replacement surgery. Cash was devastated. He was lost without June. After June's death it became clear that *The Man Comes Around* was going be the Man in Black's final album.

If Rubin was looking forward to "Hurt" appearing on the last album Johnny Cash would release during his lifetime, Cash was excited about a different song—a song that had come to him in a dream in 1993. In the dream, Cash was visiting the Queen of England in Buckingham Palace. He walked into a room to find the queen sitting on the floor, knitting and laughing. She looked up at Cash and declared, "Johnny Cash, you're just like a thorn tree in a whirlwind."

The line echoes Old Testament imagery of judgment. While the exact phrase "thorn tree in a whirlwind" isn't in the Bible, there are plenty of images of God's judgment coming as a whirlwind in the desert (Isa 40:24; Jer 23:19; Nah 1:3; Zech 7:14) or as a fire crackling through thorn bushes (Pss 58:9; 118:12; Isa 10:17). Cash read the Bible almost every day of his life. The queen's remark in the dream and the images of judgment in the Bible began to stir in Cash's mind and became the basis of a gospel song he wanted to write, a gospel song that would connect with the younger audience, who had only recently been turned on to his music. Cash searched the Bible, looking for and collecting related imagery.

By 2000, the song had become his overriding artistic passion. For years, Cash had kept his promise to Jack. He had preached the gospel through music during his entire career. And this song, "The Man Comes Around," would be his final sermon. In the last years of his life, Cash obsessed over the song, writing pages and pages of lyrics. John Carter Cash said, "It was the most important thing he had written, maybe ever, and he just loved it."[1]

———

The song opens with Cash speaking words from Revelation 6, quoting from the King James Version: "And I heard, as it were the noise of thunder, one of the four beasts saying, Come and see. And I saw, and behold a white horse." And then the singing begins:

> There's a man goin' 'round takin' names
> And he decides who to free and who to blame
> Everybody won't be treated all the same
> There'll be a golden ladder reachin' down
> When the man comes around.

From there, the apocalyptic imagery just keeps on coming. The biblical allusions and references in "The Man Comes Around" are breathtaking in their number and density. For those who want to track the biblical references and allusions, the following list is a listening guide for "The Man Comes Around":

- **"There's a man goin' around"** An image of Jesus as Judge of the living and the dead in Revelation 12:11. See also Matthew 25:31–32: "When the Son of Man comes in his glory, and all the angels with him, he will sit on his glorious throne. All the nations will be gathered before him, and he will separate the people one from another as a shepherd separates the sheep from the goats."
- **"Takin' names"** The scene of judgment from Revelation 20:12, 15: "And I saw the dead, great and small, standing before the throne, and books were opened. Another book was opened, which is the book of life. The dead were judged according to what they had done as recorded in the books. . . . Anyone whose name was not found written in the book of life was thrown into the lake of fire."

- **"A golden ladder reachin' down"**   Likely an allusion to Jacob's dream in Genesis 28. Jacob saw angels ascending and descending from a ladder reaching down from heaven.

- **"Terror in each sip"**   In Revelation 14:10, those who worship the beast must "drink the wine of God's fury, which has been poured full strength into the cup of his wrath."

- **"The potter's ground"**   A reference to the potter's field where Judas, Jesus's betrayer, committed suicide (Matt 27:10).

- **"Million angels singing"**   In Revelation 5:11, a multitude of angels worship the Lamb who sits upon the throne.

- **"Voices crying"**   The damned will find themselves in a place of "weeping and gnashing of teeth" (see Matt 8:12; 13:42). See also the rich man calling out to Abraham from his torment in Hades (Luke 16:19–24).

- **"Some are born, some are dying"**   An allusion to Jesus's comment to Nicodemus that only those who have been "born again" will enter the kingdom of God (John 3:3).

- **"Alpha and Omega"**   A description of Jesus as the "First and the Last" in Revelation (1:8; 21:6; 22:13).

- **"Kingdom come"**   An allusion to multiple references to the kingdom of God coming to earth, including in the Lord's Prayer ("Thy kingdom come") and Revelation 12:10: "Then I heard a loud voice in heaven say: 'Now have come the salvation and the power and the kingdom of our God, and the authority of his Messiah.'"

- **"Virgins are trimming their wicks"**   A reference to Jesus's parable of the ten virgins (Matt 25:1–13), a parable about watchfulness and preparation for judgment. The five wise virgins carry extra oil for their lamps so they are ready to "trim their wicks" and light their lamps when the bridegroom arrives. The five foolish virgins are unprepared with oil, so they are shut out of the festivities.

- **"Kick against the pricks"**   When Jesus appears to Saul (later Paul) on the road to Damascus, he declares, "It is hard for thee to kick against the pricks" (Acts 9:5, KJV). "Pricks" refers to goads, or sharp sticks used to prod cattle. An animal that kicked back, "against the pricks," would have incurred a self-inflicted wound.

- **"Till Armageddon"**   The location of the final battle between the hosts of Satan and the army of the Lord (Rev 16:16).

- **"Shalom"**   The Hebrew word for peace, used over two hundred times in the Old Testament.

- **"Call his chickens home"**   In the gospels, Jesus describes his longing to rescue Jerusalem from destruction as being like the protective instinct of a mother hen: "How often I have longed to gather your children together, as a hen gathers her chicks under her wings, and you were not willing" (Matt 23:37).

- **"Bow down before the throne . . . cast their golden crowns"**   In Revelation 4, the twenty-four elders lay down their crowns and worship Christ, the Lamb who sits upon the throne.

- **"Whoever is unjust let him be unjust still"**   This line and the two that follow are almost a direct quote from Revelation

22:11 (KJV): "He that is unjust, let him be unjust still: and he which is filthy, let him be filthy still: and he that is righteous, let him be righteous still."

- **"Listen to the words"**   An echo of the warning in Revelation 22:18–19: "I warn everyone who hears the words of the prophecy of this scroll: If anyone adds anything to them, God will add to that person the plagues described in this scroll. And if anyone takes words away from this scroll of prophecy, God will take away from that person any share in the tree of life and in the Holy City, which are described in this scroll."

- **"Measured hundred weight and penny pound"**   Possibly a reference to the impact of the calamitous famine described in Revelation 6:6—"Then I heard what sounded like a voice among the four living creatures, saying, 'Two pounds of wheat for a day's wages'" ("day's wages" is translated "penny" in the King James Version). Also an allusion to God's judgment upon King Belshazzar in Daniel 5:27: "You've been weighed in the balance, and found wanting." (Incidentally, the first gospel song Cash ever wrote, while stationed with the air force in Germany, was "Belshazzar.")

At the end of the song, Cash speaks one last image from Revelation's vision of the four horseman of the Apocalypse: "I heard the voice of the fourth beast say, Come and see. And I looked, and beheld a pale horse: and his name that sat on him was Death, and Hell followed with him."

Again, the depth and breadth of the biblical material used, echoed, referenced, and alluded to in "The Man Comes Around" is stunning. Only a person who read the Bible every day of their life, as Johnny Cash did, could have written such a song.

———

"The Man Comes Around" is full of the dark, rumbling, terrifying imagery of judgment day. The song is packed with allusions and words from the book of Revelation, not the book most people think of when they hear the words "good news." The Jesus in "The Man Comes Around" isn't a comforting, nurturing image. Frankly, he's terrifying. Yet this is the song Cash wanted to be his final sermon.

The Greek word for "revelation" is *apocalypse*, and that word doesn't mean judgment day or global, world-ending cataclysm. It means unveiling, as to reveal something—thus the title of the last book of the Bible, Revelation. With an apocalypse, something hidden and obscure has broken into the light, something invisible is made visible, something unseen is revealed. To witness an apocalypse is to *behold*. An apocalypse demands of us, "Look!"

The central, defining apocalypse in the book of Revelation—the unveiling that the book demands we look at—occurs in chapters 4 and 5. After John has listened to Jesus give messages to seven churches sprinkled across Asia, he is transported into the throne room of heaven, where he witnesses the hosts of heaven worshipping before the throne of God, singing, "Holy, holy, holy is the Lord God Almighty, who was, and is, and is to come" (Rev 4:8).

John then sees to the right of the throne a scroll with seven seals. A mighty angel asks of heaven in a loud voice, "Who is worthy to break the seals and open the scroll?" There is no answer, and John begins to weep. But John's lamentation is interrupted by one of the twenty-four elders, who says to him, "Do not weep! See, the Lion of the tribe of Judah, the Root of David, has triumphed. He is able to open the scroll and its seven seals" (Rev 5:5). John looks up and he sees—he beholds—the apocalypse: "Then I saw a Lamb, looking as if it had been slain, standing at the center of the throne" (Rev 5:6).

The revelation at the heart of Revelation is that the Lamb who was slain now rules the cosmos. And if we miss this revelation, everything we say about the book of Revelation can quickly slide into the ditch. Yes, the book of Revelation is filled with blood and shocking, grotesque, nightmarish imagery. This is simply the genre of Jewish apocalyptic literature; the images are not to be taken literally. What we have in Revelation is a vision of cosmic combat and victory. And the apocalypse at the heart of the book is that this grand cosmic victory is won by Jesus's death on the cross, by the Lamb who was slain. In the words of Revelation, the enemies of God are defeated "by the blood of the Lamb" (Rev 12:11). And if this seems to be a perplexing, paradoxical way to wage and win a battle, you're correct. That's precisely why we need the Apocalypse to see it.

Here's how we might understand Revelation according to the gospel according to Johnny Cash. "The Man Comes Around" *is* the Man in Black. The Jesus of "The Man Comes Around," the man of judgment going around taking names, is the same man who upon the cross stands in solidarity with the broken, lost, and cursed, the man who forgives and dies for his enemies. The Man in Black interprets "The Man Comes Around," just as the Lamb of God, who rules the cosmos by giving his life away, interprets the imagery of the book of Revelation. If the two are separated, we're going to end up with a nightmare. If we lose track of the Lamb of God, the imagery of Revelation descends into violence and blood-soaked gore. That would be a far cry from the nonviolent Jesus who prays for his torturers on the cross, "Father, forgive them!" In a similar way, if we lose track of the Man in Black, the Jesus who stands in loving solidarity with all of humanity, of course we're going to be terrified when "The Man Comes Around."

Now, that all might be true, and it helps us read the book of Revelation without having nightmares. But doesn't it avoid the pressing question? Specifically, both the book of Revelation and "The Man Comes Around" speak about a coming *judgment*. To revisit the imagery from the book of Daniel, some of us are going to be weighed and found wanting. And if that's the case, shouldn't we be worried—at least a little bit?

The issue of judgment day is a ticklish, controversial topic, both inside and outside of Christianity. Within Christianity, the debate rages about just how inclusive versus exclusive the final judgment might be. For example, some of the earliest church fathers, Origen and Gregory of Nyssa, believed that all of humanity would eventually be saved. That doesn't mean the evil and wicked get a free pass and a warm hug. Far from it. The wicked are going to shake in their shoes when the man comes around. There is going to be horrible, terrible reckoning for all the pain and suffering they have caused. God's holiness and justice demand no less. But in the view of Origen and Gregory, the judgment and punishments of God have a redemptive, restorative purpose.

If that's one end of the continuum in Christianity, the other end is the familiar fundamentalist, hellfire-and-brimstone preachers who think very few are going to be saved in the end. Most of humanity will be lost, they claim, thrown into the lake of fire to be tormented for all eternity.

Outside of Christianity, the concern about judgment day is in the exclusive claims it makes about Jesus. In an increasingly pluralistic and post-Christian world, it's scandalous to preach that every human being who has ever lived will be finally and ultimately judged by how they stand in relation to Jesus of Nazareth. As Peter says in Acts 4:12, "Salvation is found in no one else, for there is no other name under heaven given to mankind by which we must be saved."

I don't want to put my thumb down on the scale when it comes to my personal opinions on these contested subjects. You're not reading this book to get my opinions about judgment day. But I do think we need to find something to say about Jesus and judgment day that is both true to the gospel and true to Johnny Cash.

Toward the end of his life, in an interview with biographer Robert Hilburn, Cash had this to say about the song he wanted to be his final sermon to the world: "I called upon Jesus. He stood with me. I can never praise Him enough for all his blessings." Cash paused and then continued, "But I tried to praise Him with 'The Man Comes Around.' If someone is still listening to my music fifty years from now—" He paused again. "If someone is listening at all, I hope they're listening to that song."[2]

For Johnny Cash, the gospel begins and ends with Jesus. Time after time, Jesus had rescued the Man in Black from the demons that tormented him and from his worst self-destructive impulses. Jesus had forgiven and healed him, a broken, sinful man. And it was Jesus who also inspired Cash to use his music to stand with the hurt and oppressed in the world as the Man in Black. It was the same Jesus who welcomed and loved the outcasts and sinners, the Jesus who forgave his murderers upon the cross.

So the gospel according to "The Man Comes Around" boils down to this: Jesus stands before all of humanity as a sign of both love and judgment. The two are inseparable. We see evil most clearly against a backdrop of love. Love allows us to judge, to make the distinctions between good and evil, justice and oppression, hatred and peace. As Johnny Cash understands it, our lives are lived under the gaze of Jesus. His love is the grain of the universe, and all that cuts against this grain brings pain and trouble into the world. This is the judgment of God that will be revealed when the man comes around.

In the Old Testament book of Deuteronomy, Moses looked at the children of God and said, "I set before you this day life and death. Choose life." For Johnny Cash, the love he found in Jesus was this choice. In every second and in every choice, our lives are weighed and measured by it. Are we choosing life? Are we choosing love? Our answers to those questions will be our final judgment. When the man comes around, love will be the scale upon which our lives will be weighed—yours, mine, and all of humanity's.

That was the final sermon preached by Johnny Cash. Judgment day is coming, and today you stand at the crossroads. Choose love.

"THE GOSPEL ROAD"

The West Texas sun dipped behind the mesquite trees and prickly pear as I walked toward the guardhouse. Passing through the barbed-wire fences, I read once again the sign "No Hostages Shall Pass Through This Gate." This was a night when the guards patted you down when you left the prison—a random, unannounced search to look for contraband being smuggled out. The officers searched my Bible. I lifted my arms and spread my legs, so I could be patted down. I lifted each foot, so the guard behind me could see I had nothing hidden in the bottom of my socks.

Leaving the guardhouse, I glanced up at the observation tower that looked over this corner of the prison. The tower always gives me that weird, self-conscious feeling you get when you're being watched.

Watching the sun turn the sky into a kaleidoscope of reds, pinks, oranges, and yellows, I stood pensive and thoughtful. Not many people think West Texas is beautiful. It's too flat and desolate. But oh, my goodness, God has blessed us with sunsets.

As I watched the sunset, I was thinking about Steve. Steve has been coming to my Monday-night Bible study for years. He always sits in the front row. He participates a lot, and he always asks hard, probing questions. Steve is smart; he's a thinker. He looks even smarter because he wears the prison-issued frames for his glasses: big, black, horned-rim, Buddy Holly frames. Outside, in the free world, hipsters would think those bulky frames were cool. But inside the prison, they are a symbol of poverty and loneliness.

Wealth in the prison is determined by two things. First, do you have a hustle? A hustle is some job, access, or ability you possess that is of value in the prison economy. A lot of guys in my study have a garment factory hustle. Possessing a job in the garment factory, where the white clothing of the inmates is mended and cleaned, a man can wash, bleach, and starch your clothing for a price paid in the currency of the prison: either stamps or "real money" (food, often paid in increments of soup packets, as in "It's worth one soup"). Just as in the free world, fashion is a status symbol in the prison. Wealthy inmates pay men with garment factory hustles to keep their clothing clean, starched, and sparkling white. On an inmate, gray, limp clothing is an indicator of poverty.

The other, easier, more lucrative way to get money in the prison is to have loved ones in the free world deposit money into your account. Wealth in the prison means you have family members in the free world who care about you and regularly send you money. When an inmate is poor, that often is a sign he has no one in the world who cares about him, or a sign that his family is extraordinarily poor and can't send even a few dollars.

Steve's big Buddy Holly glasses told me he was poor and without family. Any inmate with money or a family quickly replaces his prison-issue glasses with designer frames. A loved one has to smuggle the frames into the prison, which is pretty easy. Your family member or friend picks out the frames you like, buys them, and then wears them to a visit. During the visit, the visitor takes off the glasses, and the inmate puts them on. Few guards notice, and if they do, they let it slide. Then a prisoner has to find a guy who has a lens-grinding hustle who will grind down your massive, prison-issue, Buddy Holly–size prescription lenses to make them fit the new designer frames your loved one just gave you. A class member in my study works this hustle, and I asked how much it cost to fit lenses. "Two soups," he said. He has fitted the glasses of every guy in my study.

Anyway, I knew Steve didn't have a lot of money. I could see that from his big glasses and dingy clothing. And I knew what that meant: no hustle perhaps, but more likely, no one in the free world who cared about him.

This was confirmed the night I stood pensively watching the sunset. During the study, I had been talking about the love of God—good, old gospel-according-to-Johnny-Cash material. God has poured out upon us massive, lavish, abundant, unmerited grace. Given the sorts of criminal backgrounds the inmates have—real "Delia's Gone" and "Folsom Prison Blues" sorts of crimes—the weight of guilt and shame the men carry in my study is crippling. So we regularly come back to this message about the grace of God, a grace given even to the very worst of sinners. It's a message that never fails to resonate. If you preach about the grace of God in a prison you're going to get some teary eyes. "God loves you," I say over and over, "No matter your past, no matter your sins."

But on this particular night, Steve raised his hand and interrupted my sermon on grace. I stopped, and Steve asked me a question that shook me to the core. "How can I believe that God loves me?" asked Steve, "when I've never had another human being tell me that they loved me?"

The room was silent, so Steve continued. "My mother never told me she loved me. My father never told me he loved me. No one, in my entire life, has ever told me that they loved me. So if I've never heard another person say that they loved me, how can I believe that God loves me?"

My heart broke, pondering what Steve had just shared. What would your life be like if no one, ever, not once, had said to you, "I love you"? What would it feel like to have never heard "I love you" from your mother or father, or from a friend or lover? What had Steve's life been like, given that he had *never* heard the words "I love you"?

That was what I was thinking about in the parking lot that night as the sun set on the horizon.

———

The biggest artistic project of Johnny Cash's career was the production of his film *The Gospel Road*, the soundtrack of which was a double LP. Filmed on location in Israel and released in 1973, *The Gospel Road* is a dramatization of the life, death, burial, and resurrection of Jesus of Nazareth, as told by Johnny Cash in narration and song:

Matthew, Mark, and Luke and John
Told about Jesus on the gospel highway
Matthew, Mark, and Luke and John
Told about Jesus on the gospel road.

Johnny and June had been talking about doing a movie about the life of Jesus ever since their first visit to Israel. During that visit, Cash carried a tape recorder with him, recording the sounds of the Holy Land along with his thoughts and impressions as he visited locations associated with events in Old and New Testaments. Those recordings were used on Cash's 1969 gospel album, *The Holy Land*. The cover of the album features Cash standing in front of the chapel on top of the Mount of the Beatitudes, north of the Sea of Galilee.

After the cancellation of *The Johnny Cash Show* in 1971, Cash began to look for another way to keep his promise to Jack. If Cash was no longer able to preach the gospel on America's TV screens, he'd reach for something bigger: the silver screen. In November 1971, Cash and his entourage landed in Tel Aviv to make a movie.

When he landed, Cash hadn't completed the script. He had some ideas for scenes he wanted to do, as well as a general plotline. The initial idea was to film the feet of Jesus in various locations while Cash narrated the gospel story in word and song. Cash hadn't signed on a large and experienced production team, something that normally would have been involved in making a feature film. He planned to bankroll and do much of the work himself, along with a group of close associates. It was an informal, improvisational approach to filmmaking, but it did give Cash 100 percent artistic control, which is exactly what he wanted. *The Gospel Road* would embody his vision.

The one experienced filmmaker on the team was Robert Elfstrom, whom Cash asked to direct the film. But even Elfstrom couldn't offer much guidance when it came to the content of the movie. When Cash called to pitch the project, Elfstrom asked what the movie would be about. "Jesus," Cash said. Elfstrom, an agnostic, asked, "Jesus who?" "Jesus *Christ!*" Cash replied.[1]

Scouting for locations, Elfstrom decided to film in and around Tiberias, on the western shore of the Sea of Galilee. The Jordan River was close by, and Jerusalem a little over a hundred miles to the south.

As Elfstrom and Cash huddled each night, selecting locations and deciding which scene to shoot, they eventually decided to do more than film Jesus's feet. They felt the movie needed more visual drama, reenactments of the gospel stories, and that required actors. Rather than hire professional actors, Cash turned to his crew and entourage, as well as recruiting some hippies who were hiking through the Holy Land. June was cast as Mary Magdalene. Cash's sister was recruited to play the mother of Jesus. And Elfstrom, the agnostic director, thanks to his beard and long hair, became Jesus. After a few weeks of shooting in Israel, Cash flew back to the States with most of the footage that would become *The Gospel Road*.

While it isn't a particularly great film, *The Gospel Road* is earnest and devout. But most importantly, if you ever want to see Cash as a straight-up gospel preacher, sharing the story of Jesus with a Bible in his hand, the closest you're going to get is *The Gospel Road*. Jack, I'm sure, would have been proud.

The gospel according to Johnny Cash in *The Gospel Road* comes out most clearly in the crucifixion and death of Jesus. After Cash narrates Jesus's final words, "It is finished," and Jesus dies, we see a series of shots showing the cross and the dying Jesus in modern locations and cities, presumably around the world. We see Jesus dying on the cross atop an office building with planes flying overhead and on city streets as cars drive past. The message is clear: this sacrifice isn't an ancient story, a legend, or a myth. This sacrifice of love is a living, contemporary reality. Nor is this offering of grace hidden away in some stuffy old church or religious institution. This sacrifice is near you, visible and available, here and everywhere—the love of God poured out in grace upon the entire world.

———

In his letter to the Ephesians, the apostle Paul begins a prayer for the church with these words: "I pray that you may have the power to comprehend" (Eph 3:18 NRSV). Paul prays that his audience be given the power to *comprehend*—to know, to believe in something. But what is that something? This: "the breadth and length and height and depth, and to know the love of Christ that surpasses knowledge." Paul's petition is that we be given the *power*, the strength, to believe how high and wide and deep is God's love for us. It's an interesting choice of words. When we hear the words *power* and *strength*, we tend to think of physical strength, the ability to lift a great weight. But in Paul's prayer, we need power of a different sort. We need the power of comprehension. The biggest, heaviest rock we have to lift in life is the knowledge of just how much God loves us.

That's what I realized that night I was watching the sunset out at the prison. You can tell others all you want about the love and grace of God. You can preach like Cash in *The Gospel Road*. But some people just can't lift that rock. Steve, for example, didn't have the strength to comprehend it. Because no one in his life had ever told him, "I love you," Steve did not find the love of God believable.

Steve is not alone. Many of us have been hurt and damaged by others. We carry lasting scars. Toxic, hurtful words have been thrown like knives at us by the very people who were supposed to care for and protect us. Or, as with Steve, the wounds come from the absence of words of love. As Johnny Cash once shared about the troubled relationship he had with his father, "He never once told me he loved me."[2] These hurtful words or deafening silences become thorns deeply embedded within our souls. We've become convinced in the deep recesses of our being—those sad, wounded places that medication and therapy often fail to reach—that we are deeply, profoundly, and permanently unlovable. We are damaged and broken beyond repair. And because of these wounds, the love of God is simply, utterly unbelievable.

So how are we to help each other gain the strength to comprehend and believe in the love of God? In his book *Life Together*, Dietrich Bonhoeffer shares this:

> Help must come from the outside. . . . God has willed that we should seek and find God's living Word in the testimony of other Christians, in the mouth of human beings. Therefore, Christians need other Christians to speak God's Word to them. They need them again and again when they become uncertain and disheartened because, living by their own resources, they cannot help themselves without cheating

themselves out of the truth. They need other Christians as bearers and proclaimers of the divine word of salvation. . . . The Christ in [our] own hearts is weaker than the Christ in the words of other Christians. [Our] own hearts are uncertain; those of [our] brothers and sisters are sure.[3]

Christ comes to us in the words of other Christians. God's love was to Steve uncertain and weak. He was cheating himself out of the truth, through no fault of his own. So help has to come to Steve, and to all us, from the outside. So every week, I stand before Steve to hug him, look him in the eyes, and say, "Steve, I love you."

We make the love of God believable when we stand before each other as sacraments of God's love. That's what I try to do for Steve each week when I say to him, "I love you." Steve lacks the strength to comprehend the love of God, so I stand before him as a visible, human, flesh-and-blood sign of that invisible reality. I become a sacrament of God's love for Steve. And slowly, drop by drop, we begin to make the love of God believable to each other. As sacraments of God's love, we give each other the strength to comprehend just how deep and wide is God's love for us.

And that is exactly what I've found so powerful about the music of Johnny Cash. In an interview, Cash was asked what he wanted to communicate in his music. His answer was simple: "Love."[4] When Johnny Cash walked out onto the stage of Folsom Prison, he was saying what I try to say to Steve every Monday night as I keep showing up, week after week, year after year: "I see you. You have not been forgotten. I love you."

The music of Johnny Cash is a sacrament that makes the love of God believable, a visible sign of an invisible reality for the broken and beaten down. The music of the Man in Black gives people the power to comprehend just how deep and wide is God's love for them.

If you doubt any of this, just listen to *At Folsom Prison*. Listen to that simple, understated introduction, "Hello, I'm Johnny Cash." Listen to the Tennessee Three start in with that unmistakable *boom-chicka-boom* sound, letting you know something is chugging toward you, just 'round that bend in the railroad tracks—a voice like no other, coming to hit you like a freight train. But mostly, listen to the audience of prisoners. Listen to the cheers of the forsaken, the lost, and the damned. They have been seen. They have not been forgotten. They have been told, "I love you."

And somewhere in that roar, if you listen for it, you'll hear the gospel according to Johnny Cash.

ACKNOWLEDGMENTS

First, a big thank you to the editorial, copyright, design, and production teams at Fortress Press for supporting me and getting this book into print.

I am not a biographer or historian, so in writing this book, I had to lean heavily upon the work of others. By far the most important work I used was Robert Hilburn's authoritative biography, *Johnny Cash: The Life* (New York: Little, Brown, 2013). This is the best book about Johnny Cash out there, and it's the very next book you should read about the Man in Black. Prior to Hilburn's work, the full story about Cash's addiction and his repeated relapses hadn't been told. Consequently, beyond being the best overall account of Cash's life, Hilburn's biography was critical to chapter 10, "Sunday Mornin' Coming Down."

Michael Streissguth's book *Johnny Cash at Folsom Prison: The Making of a Masterpiece* (Cambridge, MA: Da Capo, 2005) was my main resource for chapters 4 and 5, "At Folsom Prison" and "Greystone Chapel." If you want to read a book just about the Folsom Prison concert, this is the book to read. The book is also full of pictures, taken by Jim Marshall, of the concert. The perfect gift for the Johnny Cash fan in your life is *Johnny Cash at Folsom and San Quentin* (London: Reel Art/BMG, 2018), a stunning coffee table book of both the Folsom and San Quentin concerts featuring the photos of Jim Marshall. Streissguth's biography of Cash *Johnny Cash: The Biography* (Cambridge, MA: Da Capo, 2007), along with *Ring of Fire: The Johnny Cash Reader* (Cambridge, MA: Da Capo, 2003), an edited volume of articles about and interviews with Cash, also were very helpful.

Antonino D'Ambrosio's book *A Heartbeat and a Guitar: Johnny Cash and the Making of Bitter Tears* (New York: Nation, 2009) was a wonderful resource in writing chapter 7, "The Ballad of Ira Hayes." This is the book to read if you want to learn more about the album *Bitter Tears* and Cash's involvement in Native American advocacy.

Of course, Johnny Cash's autobiographies—*Man in Black: His Own Story in His Own Words* (Grand Rapids: Zondervan, 1976) and *Cash: The Autobiography* (New York: HarperOne, 2003)—were important resources for historical and biographical information.

Dave Urbanski's *The Man Comes Around: The Spiritual Journey of Johnny Cash* (Lake Mary, FL: Relevant Media Group, 2004) also provided me with helpful biographical information, along with a wealth of spiritual insights into the music of Johnny Cash. And a big thank you to my friend and colleague David McAnulty at Abilene Christian University for recommending to me Rodney Clapp's book *Johnny Cash and the Great American Contradiction: Christianity and the Battle for the Soul of a Nation* (Louisville: Westminster John Knox, 2008). I wanted in my book to wrestle with parts of Cash's music that pose challenges for theological reflection—namely, Cash's patriotic music and his songs about war. Clapp's book helped me immensely in framing these issues in relation to Cash's music.

John Carter Cash's *House of Cash: The Legacies of My Father, Johnny Cash* (San Rafael, CA: Insight Editions, 2011) was very helpful and would also be a wonderful gift for any Johnny Cash fan. The book is full of John Carter Cash's memories and reflections about his father and is stuffed with photos and facsimile copies of Johnny Cash's letters, lyrics, notes, drawings, and recipes.

Finally, a warm thank you to Corynn Martin and Tiffany Forsythe for their editorial help.

NOTES

INTRODUCTION: TRAINS, JESUS, AND MURDER

1. Quentin Tarantino, liner notes, *Murder*, Legacy/Columbia, 2000.
2. John Carter Cash, *House of Cash: The Legacies of My Father, Johnny Cash* (San Rafael, CA: Insight Editions, 2011), 52.
3. Rosanne Cash, "My Dad Johnny Cash," in *Cash: By the Editors of Rolling Stone*, ed. Jason Fine (New York: Crown, 2004), 13.

CHAPTER 1: "I AM BOUND FOR THE PROMISED LAND"

1. Johnny Cash, *Man in Black: His Own Story in His Own Words* (Grand Rapids: Zondervan, 1976), 47.
2. J. C. Cash, *House of Cash*, 28.
3. J. Cash, *Man in Black*, 42–43.
4. J. C. Cash, *House of Cash*, 31.
5. Robert Hilburn, *Johnny Cash: The Life* (New York: Little, Brown, 2013), 17.
6. J. Cash, *Man in Black*, 243–44.

CHAPTER 2: "I WALK THE LINE"

1. Hilburn, *Johnny Cash*, 104.
2. Hilburn, *Johnny Cash*, 104.
3. Mikal Gilmore, "The Man in Black" in *Cash: By the Editors of Rolling Stone*, ed. Jason Fine (New York: Crown, 2004), 24.
4. Gilmore, "Man in Black," 24.

5. Michael Streissguth, *Ring of Fire: The Johnny Cash Reader* (Cambridge, MA: Da Capo, 2003), 151.

CHAPTER 3: "THE MAN IN BLACK"

1. William Stringfellow, *A Private and Public Faith* (Eugene: Wipf and Stock, 1999), 43.
2. Dave Urbanski, *The Man Comes Around: The Spiritual Journey of Johnny Cash* (Lake Mary, FL: Relevant Media, 2004), xx.
3. Urbanski, *The Man Comes Around*, 189.
4. Dietrich Bonhoeffer, *London, 1933–1935*, ed. Keith W. Clements, trans. Isabel Best, Dietrich Bonhoeffer Works 13 (Minneapolis: Fortress Press, 2007), 344.
5. David Benjamin Blower, *Sympathy for Jonah: Reflections on Humiliation, Terror and the Politics of Enemy-Love* (Eugene: Resource, 2016), 39–40.

CHAPTER 4: "FOLSOM PRISON BLUES"

1. Michael Streissguth, *Johnny Cash at Folsom Prison: The Making of a Masterpiece* (Cambridge, MA: Da Capo, 2005), 93.
2. Gilmore, "Man in Black," 40.
3. Robert Hilburn, *Johnny Cash: The Life* (New York: Little, Brown, 2013), 79.
4. Streissguth, *Johnny Cash at Folsom Prison*, 89.
5. Streissguth, *Johnny Cash at Folsom Prison*, 40.
6. Streissguth, *Johnny Cash at Folsom Prison*, 20.
7. Streissguth, *Johnny Cash at Folsom Prison*, 13–14.
8. For more on this, see my book *Stranger God: Meeting Jesus in Disguise* (Minneapolis: Fortress Press, 2017).

CHAPTER 5: "GREYSTONE CHAPEL"

1. Hilburn, *Johnny Cash*, 439.
2. Streissguth, *Johnny Cash at Folsom Prison*, 67.
3. Hilburn, *Johnny Cash*, 330.
4. Streissguth, *Johnny Cash at Folsom Prison*, 115.
5. Streissguth, *Johnny Cash at Folsom Prison*, 118.
6. Streissguth, *Johnny Cash at Folsom Prison*, 165.

7. Jim Marshall, *Johnny Cash at Folsom and San Quentin* (London: Reel Art/BMG, 2018), 81.

CHAPTER 6: "SAN QUENTIN"

1. Gilmore, "Man in Black," 40.
2. Hilburn, *Johnny Cash*, 354.
3. Gilmore, "Man in Black," 40.
4. Hilburn, *Johnny Cash*, 354–55.
5. Walter Brueggemann, *The Message of the Psalms: A Theological Commentary* (Minneapolis: Augsburg, 2007), 51–52.

CHAPTER 7: "THE BALLAD OF IRA HAYES"

1. Antonino D'Ambrosio, *A Heartbeat and a Guitar: Johnny Cash and the Making of Bitter Tears* (New York: Nation, 2009), 171.
2. Charla Bear, "American Indian Boarding Schools Haunt Many," *Morning Edition* (NPR), May 12, 2008, https://tinyurl.com/y23arqtx.
3. Bear, "American Indian Boarding Schools."
4. Rodney Clapp, *Johnny Cash and the Great American Contradiction: Christianity and the Battle for the Soul of a Nation* (Louisville: Westminster John Knox, 2008), 98.
5. Bob Ekblad, *Reading the Bible with the Damned* (Louisville: Westminster John Knox, 2005).

CHAPTER 8: "GIVE MY LOVE TO ROSE"

1. Hilburn, *Johnny Cash*, 123.
2. Hilburn, *Johnny Cash*, 123.
3. J. C. Cash, *House of Cash*, 19.
4. Richard Beck, *Stranger God: Meeting Jesus in Disguise* (Minneapolis: Fortress Press, 2017), 240–41.
5. Joel Lovell, "George Saunders's Advice to Graduates," *New York Times*, July 31, 2013, https://tinyurl.com/y2292by6.

CHAPTER 9: "THE LEGEND OF JOHN HENRY'S HAMMER"

1. J. Cash, *Man in Black*, 23.
2. Quentin Tarantino, liner notes, *Murder*, Legacy/Columbia, 2000.

3. Francis, *Evangelii Gaudium: Apostolic Exhortation on the Proclamation of the Gospel in Today's World*, November 24, 2013, https://tinyurl.com/mvreyv4.

CHAPTER 10: "SUNDAY MORNING COMING DOWN"

1. Streissguth, *Ring of Fire*, 150.
2. Matt Diehl, "Remembering Johnny," *Rolling Stone*, June 25, 2018, https://tinyurl.com/y63qefx9.
3. Hilburn, *Johnny Cash*, 313.
4. Hilburn, *Johnny Cash*, 277.
5. J. C. Cash, *House of Cash*, 41.
6. Hilburn, *Johnny Cash*, 397.
7. Jason Fine, ed., *Cash: By the Editors of Rolling Stone* (New York: Crown, 2004), 211.
8. More of this story is recounted in my book *Reviving Old Scratch: Demons and the Devil for Doubters and the Disenchanted* (Minneapolis: Fortress Press, 2016).
9. Hilburn, *Johnny Cash*, 387.
10. Hilburn, *Johnny Cash*, 387.
11. Gilmore, "Man in Black," 37.
12. J. C. Cash, *House of Cash*, 22.
13. J. Cash, *Man in Black*, 139.
14. J. Cash, *Man in Black*, 170–71.
15. J. C. Cash, *House of Cash*, 22.
16. Streissguth, *Ring of Fire*, 151.

CHAPTER 11: "RAGGED OLD FLAG"

1. Rosanne Cash, Kathy Cash, Cindy Cash, Tara Cash, and John Carter Cash, post on Rosanne Cash's Facebook page, August 16, 2017, http://tinyurl.com/yx8okela.
2. See James Davison Hunter, *To Change the World: The Irony, Tragedy, and Possibility of Christianity in the Late Modern World* (Oxford University Press, 2010).
3. The election of Donald Trump in 2016 has muddied these waters. After Trump's victory, a great deal of commentary asked if the Democratic Party had lost touch with its traditional working-class, Rust Belt

constituencies—organized labor in particular. For example, see Mark Lilla, *Once and Future Liberal: The End of Identity Politics* (Harper, 2017). It is argued that since the nineties, Democrats have shifted away from their traditional focus on class to focus upon the politics of identity (e.g., gender, race, sexuality). Donald Trump's economic nationalism, it is argued, stepped into this vacuum, allowing him to pick up critical votes in Rust Belt states. Thus, in 2016, Donald Trump's "Make America Great Again" campaign was *doubly* nostalgic, evoking the cultural and values consensus of the Republican Party, as well as nostalgia for economic dominance, especially in the manufacturing sector, which had been the traditional appeal of Democrats.

4. Gilmore, "Man in Black," 43.

5. Ralph Gleason, "Johnny Cash Meets Dick Nixon" in *Cash: By the Editors of Rolling Stone,* ed. Jason Fine (New York: Crown, 2004), 103.

CHAPTER 12: "DRIVE ON"

1. Hilburn, *Johnny Cash*, 374.

2. Harvey Shapiro, "A Conversation with Jimmy Carter," *New York Times*, June 19, 1977, https://tinyurl.com/yyam9r22.

3. Clapp, *Johnny Cash and the Great American Contradiction*, 103.

4. *VH1 Storytellers*, performance by Johnny Cash and Willie Nelson, dir. Michael Simon, season 2, episode 3, American Recordings, May 12, 1997.

5. Richard A. Kulka, *Trauma and the Vietnam War Generation: Report of Findings from the National Vietnam Veterans Readjustment Study* (Abingdon, UK: Routledge, 2013).

6. Jessica J. Fulton et al., "The Prevalence of Posttraumatic Stress Disorder in Operation Enduring Freedom/Operation Iraqi Freedom (OEF/OIF) Veterans: A Meta-Analysis," *Journal of Anxiety Disorders* 31 (April 2015): 98–107.

7. Streissguth, *Johnny Cash*, 258.

CHAPTER 13: "DELIA'S GONE"

1. Hilburn, *Johnny Cash*, 511.

2. Hilburn, *Johnny Cash,* 540.

3. John Garst, *Delia* (Northfield, MN: Loomis House, 2012), 21.

4. Hilburn, *Johnny Cash*, 544.

5. Hilburn, *Johnny Cash*, 544.

6. Clapp, *Johnny Cash and the Great American Contradiction*, 103.

7. Quentin Tarantino, liner notes, *Murder*, Legacy/Columbia, 2000.

CHAPTER 14: "HURT"

1. Marshall, *Johnny Cash at Folsom and San Quentin*, 116.

2. "The Alternative Jesus: Psychedelic Christ," *Time*, June 21, 1971, https://tinyurl.com/y34vj7cl.

3. Thomas Frank, "Why Johnny Can't Dissent," in *Commodify Your Dissent: Salvos from* The Baffler, ed. Thomas Frank and Matt Weiland (New York: Norton, 1997), 34.

4. Hilburn, *Johnny Cash*, 546–47.

5. Hilburn, *Johnny Cash*, 547.

6. "Rolling Stone Readers Pick the Top 10 Greatest Cover Songs," *Rolling Stone*, June 25, 2018, https://tinyurl.com/y5lxdcfv.

7. *Rolling Stone*, "Rolling Stone Readers Pick the Top 10."

8. Gilmore, "Man in Black," 50.

9. J. C. Cash, *House of Cash*, 27.

10. Gilmore, *Cash*, 27.

11. Mark Love, "Johnny Cash, Outlaw, Sufferer, and the Gospel," *Deiliberations* (blog), February 18, 2014, https://tinyurl.com/y34aj7wm.

12. Mark Love, "Sufferer, Saint or Sinner? Johnny Cash and the Gospel," *Tokens Show* blog, October 10, 2018, https://tinyurl.com/y5zkg7fg.

13. J. C. Cash, *House of Cash*, 22.

CHAPTER 15: "THE MAN COMES AROUND"

1. Hilburn, *Johnny Cash*, 590.

2. Hilburn, *Johnny Cash*, 600.

EPILOGUE: "THE GOSPEL ROAD"

1. Hilburn, *Johnny Cash*, 408.

2. Gilmore, "Man in Black," 25.

3. Dietrich Bonhoeffer, *Life Together* (Minneapolis: Fortress Press, 2015), 6.

4. Streissguth, *Ring of Fire*, 147.

The Man in Black
Words and Music by John R. Cash
Copyright © 1971 Song Of Cash, Inc.
Copyright Renewed
All Rights Administered by BMG Rights Management (US) LLC
All Rights Reserved Used by Permission
Reprinted by Permission of Hal Leonard LLC

Folsom Prison Blues
Words and Music by John R. Cash
Copyright © 1956 House Of Cash, Inc.
Copyright Renewed
All Rights Administered by BMG Rights Management (US) LLC
All Rights Reserved Used by Permission
Reprinted by Permission of Hal Leonard LLC

San Quentin
Words and Music by John R. Cash
Copyright © 1969 Song Of Cash Music
Copyright Renewed
All Rights Administered by BMG Rights Management (US) LLC
All Rights Reserved Used by Permission
Reprinted by Permission of Hal Leonard LLC

Give My Love to Rose

Words and Music by John R. Cash

Copyright © 1957 Song Of Cash Music

Copyright Renewed

All Rights Administered by BMG Rights Management (US) LLC

All Rights Reserved Used by Permission

Reprinted by Permission of Hal Leonard LLC

Give My Love to Rose

Words and Music by JOHNNY R. CASH

Copyright © 1965 (Renewed) CHAPPELL & CO., INC.

All Rights Reserved

Used by Permission of ALFRED MUSIC

Sunday Mornin' Coming Down

Words and Music by Kris Kristofferson

Copyright © 1969 Combine Music Corp.

Copyright Renewed

All Rights Administered by Sony/ATV Music Publishing LLC, 424
    Church Street, Suite 1200, Nashville, TN 37219

International Copyright Secured All Rights Reserved

Reprinted by Permission of Hal Leonard LLC

Ragged Old Flag

Words and Music by John R. Cash

Copyright © 1974 Song Of Cash Music

Copyright Renewed

All Rights Administered by BMG Rights Management (US) LLC

Drive On

Words and Music by John R. Cash

The Man Comes Around

Words and Music by John R. Cash

Gospel Road

Words and Music by John R. Cash

The Ballad of Ira Hayes

Words and Music by PETER LA FARGE

Legend of John Henry's Hammer

Traditional

Arranged by JUNE CARTER and JOHNNY R. CASH

All God's Children Ain't Free

Words and Music by JOHNNY R. CASH

Hurt

Written by Trent Reznor (ASCAP)

TRAINS, JESUS, AND MURDER

THE GOSPEL ACCORDING TO JOHNNY CASH